CABBAGES & ROSES

a life in fabric

CABBAGES & ROSES

a life in fabric

BRING COLOUR, PATTERN AND
TEXTURE INTO YOUR HOME

CHRISTINA STRUTT

CICO BOOKS
LONDON NEW YORK

Editor: Sophie Devlin

Designer: Rian Davies

Art director: Sally Powell

Head of production: Patricia Harrington

Production manager: Gordana Simakovic

Senior commissioning editor: Annabel Morgan

Creative director: Leslie Harrington

Publisher: Cindy Richards

Photography: James Scott-Long
and Belle Daughtry

Additional photography: Andrew Beasley,
Simon Brown, Antony Crolla, Lucinda Symons,
Edina van der Wyck and courtesy of
Ashley Wilde

For photography credits, see page 189

Illustrations: Tiffany Dunlop

Published in 2022 by CICO Books
An imprint of Ryland Peters & Small Ltd
20–21 Jockey's Fields
London WC1R 4BW
and
341 E 116th St
New York, NY 10029
www.rylandpeters.com

10 9 8 7 6 5 4 3 2

A CIP catalog record for this book is available
from the Library of Congress and the British
Library.

ISBN 978 1 800651 03 6

Printed in China

Contents

In the beginning there was Bees

At the age of 19, I had the good fortune to find myself working in the art department at British *Vogue*. The offices were situated in Hanover Square in central London, and at that time they were not in the least bit glamorous. The magazine's editor, Beatrix Miller, used to call me "the office lunatic". I had indeed a somewhat chaotic career and got into quite a few scrapes, from which I had to be rescued by Miss Miller and on one occasion by the Condé Nast lawyers. But that is a long story for another book…

After three years, I was offered the job of assistant to *Vogue*'s Living editor, Judy Brittain. I was not one for a plan, nor did I have any discernible ambition, but serendipity led me to be in the right place at the right time. I learned from the best and found myself in the drawing rooms, bedrooms and gardens of the world's most beautiful houses, working with the most talented photographers of the time. My job was to style and help direct, though not much of either was ever required of me. Not having a house of my own, I was very happy to imbibe the beauty and brilliance of my surroundings. I stored up these memories and waited for the right time, which came 20 years later when Cabbages & Roses was born.

It began with my friend Brigette Buchanan and I deciding to make a newly printed fabric that would have the atmosphere of age and a faded timeworn appearance. Our first design was called Bees. Taken from a scrap of old fabric, it featured a central bloom surrounded by garlands of flowers in a heavenly worn-out pink and faded greens. The ubiquitous Hatley rose print soon followed and remains our best-selling design. Impressively variable in appearance depending on the base cloth and colourway, the floral motif is derived from the rose featured in the Bees print and has become a modern classic, at once striking and elegant. These two relatively simple designs were followed by a multitude of cozy, sophisticated and joyful patterns in many colourways, all printed onto pure linen and made into an assortment of ever-changing accessories.

Somehow, when I first laid eyes on a finished product, straight off the press, I felt a twinge of disappointment — it always looked too new and lacking in personality. Often, we would wash and line dry the fabrics before they were made into clothes and accessories, which gave them an added pre-loved dimension. Our fabrics are never printed in large quantities, for a good reason. I have seen production lines in factories and the resulting stock numbering thousands, and I would never want to make so many things that were not special and were destined for landfill somewhere in the world. To counteract this, we have always produced everything in small quantities, believing it is better to run out than to be left with unwanted stock.

For 22 years now, Cabbages & Roses has supplied fabrics to thousands of people all over the world. It gives me great pleasure to see the houses and bodies swathed in our designs, both in clothing and in interiors. Over time, we have frequently updated and reinvented our designs, accumulating many photographs along the way. So it was inevitable that one day those images should become part of a book explaining the inherent beauty, versatility and friendliness of our fabrics. So here it is, a reference book showing how our fabric designs have been and can be used. I hope it will introduce you to a gentle world of faded florals, delicate stripes, voluminous blooms and simple linens.

I am writing this in July 2021, in the midst of a global pandemic that has confined us to our homes for the best part of 18 months. Although we are becoming used to this new way of life, nothing could have prepared us for it. Our houses and apartments have now become our whole world. Whereas clothes would have been the most important items in our shopping baskets in the past, now it is home-related purchases that make up the bulk of the retail economy.

It is marvellous that CICO Books, the publisher of our previous books, has agreed with me that these words and pictures should be printed on actual paper rather than viewed on a screen. Welcome to a photographic journey celebrating 22 years of Cabbages & Roses, the essence of the brand and the affection it has inspired.

PREVIOUS PAGE LEFT In my London apartment above our first shop on Langton Street in Chelsea, the sitting room was decorated with our Mary wallpaper in lilac. It was a bold choice for a small space, but more life enhancing than white walls.

OPPOSITE TOP I keep pencils in pots and jars in every room of my house.
OPPOSITE BOTTOM It all began with Bees, a pattern based on an ancient inherited quilt that was much beloved by my friend and partner, Brigette Buchanan. Hatley, seen on the pillow, was our second fabric and remains a bestseller. LEFT Bees, printed onto a piece of antique linen, here acts as a temporary curtain.

The Simple Life

Cabbages & Roses started its life at the beginning of this century. In those early years, there were wars, financial crashes and anticipated worldwide computer chaos as the century turned. London had a new Millennium Dome, a rather wobbly Millennium Bridge and a new art gallery called the Tate Modern. Meanwhile, somewhere in the English countryside, oblivious to the goings-on in the world, Brigette and I were yearning for a return to the simple life of faded floral fabrics and handmade clothing, and establishing a business run on our own terms.

Before the internet was part of our lives, we started our tiny enterprise by attending local shows, selling not much more than a few cushion covers and handmade skirts. It was here that we first benefitted from the astonishing power of magazine coverage. The lovely Vanessa Arbuthnott – herself a fabric designer – bought one of our cushions, and by a happy coincidence *Country Living* magazine was photographing her house that very day. The cushion was featured in the photoshoot, and as a result of that tiny amount of exposure, Cabbages & Roses left the kitchen table (metaphorically speaking) and was launched into the world.

Brigette and I decided to set up a little showroom at Brook Cottage, my home in Somerset, in what was once my children's nursery. Suddenly strangers from all over the world were making appointments to come and visit us, browse our wares and order fabric from a choice of two designs, Bees and Hatley.

There followed many more magazine articles, and our first book, *Vintage Chic*, was published in 2003. Naturally, the book featured photographs of Brook Cottage, both indoors and out. We revisited the house for subsequent volumes – the same rooms and the same garden but redecorated, re-planted and re-invented each time there was a book to produce. Here it is again, popping up here and there in this book but in different clothes. The house has been so much part of Cabbages & Roses, and my home for more than 40 years. It has adapted and changed, grown and contracted, but throughout the decades it has remained a pleasing constant in our lives.

OPPOSITE These wall-mounted shelves in the kitchen at Brook Cottage are a vintage find and contain a medley of mostly pink lustreware china. Many pieces have been cracked and mended, which makes me love them all the more. Rarely do we use any of these pieces, they are simply decorative. Throughout the spring and summer, I fill the house with fresh flowers and greenery. ABOVE This "James Galway" rose by David Austin Roses is a luxurious and beautiful pink climber, whose blooms last from June to October. It is currently planted against one of the pavilion supports, though it will have to be moved this autumn to somewhere more suitable.

The publication of *Vintage Chic* coincided with our first foray into the world of retail in London. We took the lease of a charming "cottage" premises on Langton Street at the wrong end of the world-famous King's Road in Chelsea. The shop was laid out on three floors with a miniature garden at the back – a fragment of countryside in the middle of the city. It seemed we were doing the right thing at the right time, with providence still guiding the progress of our fledgling company. The power of the press kept us going, as articles appeared in many national and international magazines and newspapers.

The shop became a well-known destination, with customers arriving from all over the world – some even came straight from Heathrow Airport, leaving a taxi waiting outside. Years later, when we licensed our wares in Japan, our partners there built a shop modelled on our Langton Street idyll. It was always a pleasure to visit this home from home on the other side of the world. In the time that followed, another three London shops were opened in Battersea, Notting Hill and Mayfair. In 2011, my daughter Kate Howells, who had been instrumental in Cabbages & Roses from the outset, set off on her own adventure living in Hong Kong and New York with her new husband Christopher.

In 2006 we had become part of the Jigsaw group and were kindly offered spaces in some of the firm's stores, on high streets from Fulham to Edinburgh and Guildford to Glasgow – in all, 23 of these mini Cabbages & Roses shops were opened. During this time, we also opened three shops in Japan and agreed to a license with the clothing brand Uniqlo (which displayed Cabbages & Roses designs in its store windows all over the world), all while producing seasonal clothing collections and writing four books.

Somehow, we survived this rollercoaster ride almost intact. Our early successes had enabled us to expand rapidly, and during this time we had spread our unsteady wings rather too far. However, I feel sure that none of the spirit of Cabbages & Roses was lost during this speedy expansion and we learned some valuable lessons. With the benefit of experience, we were able to regroup and start again for the umpteenth time, a great deal wiser than before.

TOP RIGHT From the beginning, our branding was as simple as a hand-stamped logo on a brown paper bag. BOTTOM RIGHT In Prague many years ago, I stumbled upon an old-fashioned tobacconist who sold miniature matches. He kindly shared the source and we have used these tiny little matches as a calling card ever since. OPPOSITE The fireplace in one of our shops on Sydney Street in Chelsea.

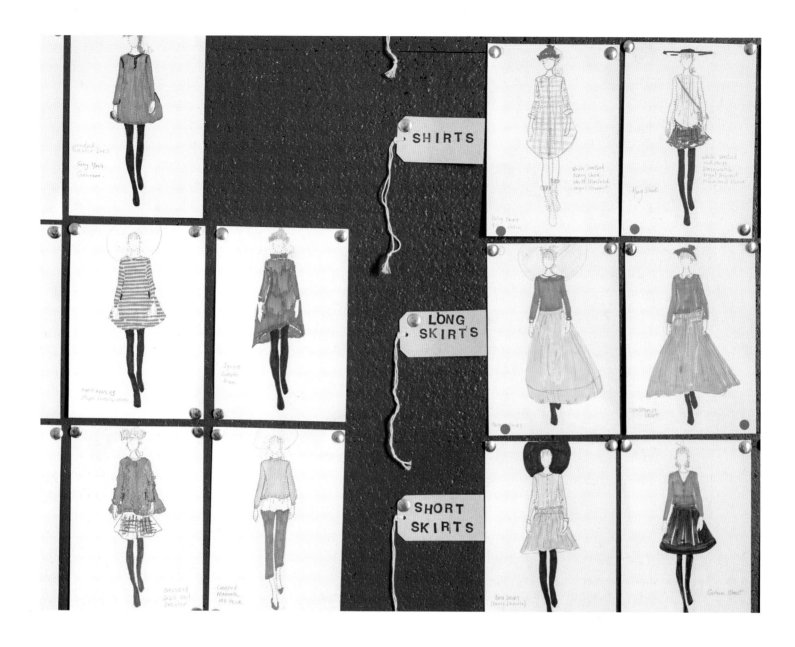

Independent again in 2014, we set up a new Chelsea store at 121 and 123 Sydney Street, a pair of buildings dating from 1810. Just up the road was the lovely St Luke's Church, where Charles Dickens had married Catherine Hogarth in 1836. At our new London base, we established two shops side by side, one for homewares and furnishing fabrics and one for clothing, both run by charming and beautiful "Cabbage Roses".

Soon, both buildings were filled with parties and celebrations and had a wonderful atmosphere; we were bent on pleasing our customers rather than on financial gain, of which there was little. Our independence meant everything to us. We were once more in charge of our own destiny, and more importantly in charge of what we made and how we made it. We were guided by a simple philosophy, with care for the environment, our staff and our suppliers always at the centre of our work.

ABOVE Before we left London in December 2018, this drawing board covered an entire wall in our Chelsea office, where all the designing was done. Many a happy day was spent there creating lovely things for Cabbages & Roses with my assistant designer, Violet Dent. OPPOSITE LEFT In our new shop in Bruton in Somerset, white and green flowers and foliage from the garden at Brook Cottage make a charming display against our Hatley wallpaper in the dove colourway. TOP RIGHT AND BOTTOM RIGHT Fabric and wallpaper samples in the Bruton shop.

OPPOSITE LEFT We stock a range of handmade cotton trims to complement our fabrics. Often we have beautiful vintage books for sale, such as this pink scrapbook. RIGHT A mannequin dressed for the garden.

OVERLEAF The kitchen window at Brook Cottage has curtains made from Tulips & Roses. There are thick walls on either side of the window seat, one of which is covered in pink decorative plates.

Starting Afresh

Thankfully, just as life and business became too difficult for me to manage, Kate and Christopher returned to England in 2017. It was at this point that I placed Cabbages & Roses in their capable hands and took a back seat, although I still design our clothing and fabric collections and write the occasional book. It is refreshing to have young and gregarious partners, who bring life and enthusiasm to what we produce. Kate and Christopher have a very different eye to mine, which is excellent for a fabric and clothing business. I am in awe of all they do and achieve, seemingly so easily and with such flair.

The year 2018 was a turning point in our history. Facing high business taxes and competition from thousands of clothing stores that could offer far cheaper options, we made the heartbreaking decision to leave London. This was made easier by the prospect of opening a new shop back in Somerset, the birthplace of Cabbages & Roses. This is where we find ourselves now, with a huge and beautiful space in the middle of the picturesque town of Bruton. The joy of not having to commute to London once a week, not to mention the reduction in our carbon footprint, has given us all a new lease of life, and the experience of living and working locally is truly life changing.

Our new store was once a car repair workshop, with skylights set in the high ceiling. It was the perfect blank canvas for our wares. For the first time in our history, all our fabric designs can be seen in one place, occupying the main wall in our "Cabberdashery" inspired by old-fashioned suppliers of passementerie, ribbons and bows. It is the greatest pleasure to advise our customers on choices of fabrics and trims and we welcome long afternoons of interior design decisions in this charming environment with all 160 fabric samples to hand.

Some of customers are solely interested in homewares and fabrics, while others are more familiar with our twice-yearly clothing collections. Happily, with our Bruton store, we are introducing each of these two groups to the other side of our business, as there is nothing quite like a unique retail environment to reveal the true beauty and soul of the full range of Cabbages & Roses' products.

However, it is with our fabrics and home collections that my heart truly lies. Home has always been the most important element of my life; it is the steadying hand that comforts, cossets, entertains and shelters me from the world. There is nothing that makes me quite so happy as rearranging, renewing and fussing over a recently bought antique plate or a newly wallpapered room. Now that we have all had a chance to grow reacquainted with our homes, there seems no better time than now to share our photographs, taken during the past 22 years of designing, developing, recolouring and reinventing Cabbages & Roses fabrics.

Kate and Christopher now live just 15 minutes from the Bruton store in their magnificent 18th-century house, a former priory. They knew they were taking on a mammoth task when they bought this historic building, but they were certain that it was going to be their "forever" house. They decided to take the renovation project slowly and sort out all the structural elements of the building before redecorating the interiors. The Priory's huge and elegant Georgian windows, which are the antithesis to my tiny casements at Brook Cottage, make a splendid focal point for a display of Cabbages & Roses' fabrics and wallpapers, as you will see throughout the visual journey presented in this book.

The photographs show the progress we have made since our earliest beginnings. They also show the versatility of our colours and patterns and how the gentle presence of beautiful fabrics can bring a room to life, thus underlining the importance of good design. As well as printed linens, we also love the simplicity and elegance of pure plain linen, especially in an environment where other components are doing most of the work, be it wallpaper, busy patterns on sofas, beautiful paintings or just white walls and floors. There can be drama even in an all-white room.

We have divided the chapters by colour, each one presenting an entirely different aspect to decoration. I hope that this book will be an inspiration to our readers and a great help in making decisions when it comes to decorating your own spaces.

Charcoal Whites

CHARCOAL ON NATURAL AND CHARCOAL ON WHITE

Versatility is key when producing a fabric design, whether it is for a simple tablecloth or a magnificent set of drapes. The gentle tones of charcoal printed onto a natural linen base cloth complement a muted, elegant approach to decoration.

Popular for minimalist schemes, the charcoal colourway provides warmth without detracting from simple furnishings. Our designs vary from beautifully drawn and shaded all-over florals to the India Rose print, which marries the intricate vertical lines of Eastern sensibilities with the florals of pastoral England. There are also more restrained ditsy prints such as New Penny – perfect for a curtain lining or valance.

The same charcoal prints are also available on a white ground, which shows them off in a different light. This new addition is our most contemporary colourway working in urban and rural settings alike. I find it particularly pleasing when used in an all-white room.

Layering: Florals and Stripes

Nearly all our designs feature flowers of one sort or another, and the idea of using florals mechanically printed onto a flat surface to enhance the interiors of predominantly urban spaces makes complete sense to me. There has never been a culture that did not appreciate the beauty of flowers, both in their real form, in paintings and in decoration of every sort.

The period in which printed fabrics became widely available in Britain coincided with the Industrial Revolution. In the small terraced/row houses built especially for the new urban workforce, it became affordable to adorn windows with cotton florals and striped ticking curtains, which had formerly been the preserve of the rich country dwellers. Cities were growing rapidly, and farms and gardens were disappearing from the lives of the urban population. The need for a smattering of nature and colour within the home to uplift the spirit is entirely understandable, it always has been and always will be.

Chintzy florals were the mainstay of the quintessential English country-house style. These colourful motifs, mostly Indian in origin, adorned the most elegant drawing rooms and bedrooms of England and France. Many fabric patterns of today are adapted from these ancient designs, which were painted with delicate brush strokes using an infinite variety of deep, rich hues.

Although there was a moment, in our recent history, when we were all urged to "chuck out the chintz" and decorate our homes in various shades of taupe instead, and to purchase furniture and furnishings emanating from exactly the same source worldwide, this was a fad that had a thankfully temporary impact on our interior choices. Now that we are aware of the effect that cheap mass production has had and is having on the environment, it is as well to not follow fashion, lest you find that the investment that you have made in furnishings becomes obsolete within months of completion.

PAGE 20 The plain white walls and beautiful Georgian windows give this room an elegant feel. The curtain is Cabbages & Roses' Charlotte design in charcoal, printed onto white linen cloth. Our linen fabric is now woven for us in the UK, which reduces our carbon footprint substantially. Black-toned furniture and accessories, some contemporary and some antique, complete the scheme, with an injection of fresh green leaves from the azalea plant.

PREVIOUS PAGES A collage comprising several of our charcoal prints together with a selection of vintage black and white photographs and other ephemera in complementary tones.

OPPOSITE This bedroom demonstrates that even full-blown roses can have a masculine edge. The charcoal posies of Paris Rose are strewn across the bed linen, which could be reversed to display the Jolly Stripe lining instead for a different effect. The overall look would be more contemporary in a room devoid of decorative artefacts. In this more traditional setting, pictures and prints, a bird cage and other curiosities play cameo parts.

I believe it is much better to find your own style and display it with confidence in your home. In particular, I would always recommend that you invest in pieces that you will love forever, or at least until they are threadbare and need to be repaired or replaced.

I cannot deny the thrill of a change in a room, but this can come from a new set of cushion covers, or from one-of-a-kind antiques that will transform and uplift. Be creative – instead of buying new, move your furniture around, rearrange the pictures and update the upholstery. When something new is absolutely necessary, choose with care and buy the very best you can, always making sure it is something that you will love forever.

The beauty of charcoal florals when printed onto a buff natural linen is that they work well with an assortment of wall colours. A deep, rich yellow on the walls, adorned with black- and gilt-framed pictures, will have an entirely different effect compared with the same room painted in a grey-blue shade. With so many ethical paint companies to choose from, the available choices will be innumerable. There are probably thousands of whites and off-whites to choose from, each

one offering something the others do not. As long as there is either a connection or a pleasing contrast, many colours will work happily together, including some combinations that you may not have considered before. Start with colour cards, which can be ordered through the post, then buy sample pots. If possible, paint several pieces of wood or card large enough to give you an idea of what the colour will look like once applied to the walls. Colours can appear startlingly different as the sun moves around the sky, so consider how your chosen hues reflect the morning and afternoon light, and artificial light as well. Use your fabric samples in the same way, looking at them with the paint colours in different areas of the room.

For each of our floral fabrics, there is always a stripe or smaller print that can be used in conjunction for linings, chair coverings and cushions. An overtly floral scheme can be diluted with the addition of various stripes in a matching or co-ordinating colourway. Our handsome Jolly Stripe is an adaptable print that works beautifully with all our charcoal designs, whether it is printed on pure white linen or our natural-coloured version. Used as a main fabric in a room, it is contemporary, stylish and tasteful at the same time. It is equally beautiful when used to line a floral curtain or to make a bed valance or cushion cover. Wherever they appear, stripes will hold their own and please the eye in an understated, elegant manner.

OPPOSITE Paris Rose is seen here in a different situation at the seaside house of designer Atlanta Bartlett, who has used it for a quilted bedcover lined with a bold black and white check. The simple grey of the Toile de Poulet print on the curtains works well in this room whose walls have been clad in wooden tongue-and-groove panelling. ABOVE LEFT An assortment of cushions in Hatley, Paris Rose and French Toile is made cohesive by a unified colour palette.

I do love a colour-co-ordinated room, though I am not keen on the matchy-matchy look unless it is in a traditional toile de Jouy room, where I believe you cannot really have enough. The beauty of producing several designs in the same colourway is that they will mostly work companionably together. Even if the colour does not change, a variety of motifs can be introduced into a room.

In the early days of Cabbages & Roses, when every colour used in a pattern required a separate silk screen to be manufactured, it made more economical sense to design single-colour prints, with intricate shading, scratching and linework – as if drawn in pen and ink – to give the fabric interest and texture. The single-coloured designs have continued, even though modern printing processes negate the need to produce a screen for each colour. Nowadays it is a matter of choice rather than an economical decision.

For the greatest magical transformation of a room, wallpaper is the most pleasing purchase possible. An expanse of pattern on a wall immediately alters the essence of the space, giving a room an entirely new personality. When we transfer one of our fabric designs to wallpaper, the texture in the drawing becomes even more important.

LEFT AND BELOW The walls of this luxurious bedroom have been papered with Hatley in charcoal, with full-length, heavily gathered curtains in French Toile. The armchair is upholstered in Toile de Poulet and the bedcover is made from Three-Inch Stripe in charcoal on natural linen. The shiny black painted floor and freestanding enamel bathtub add to the contemporary air.

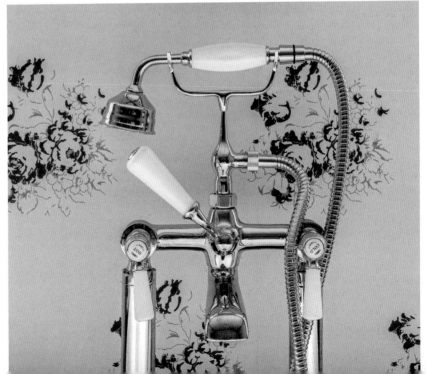

With paper, we cannot rely on the weave of the linen fabric to give the pattern a sense of depth and an organic, uneven appearance. I much prefer an entire room to be papered, rather than the half-hearted idea of having a feature wall, which to me is a waste of time and paper. I feel that if you rely on just one wall to bring pattern into a room, leaving the other three devoid of attention, nothing is gained – in fact, it would be better to do nothing at all. Equally, if your space is small, do not imagine that you can only use small prints. Large-scale designs (within reason) and bold colours can make a small room infinitely more interesting.

ABOVE Cabbages & Roses' Jolly Stripe is a ticking of the sort often found on old French mattresses. Although the fabric is printed in vertical lines, this simple blind/shade has been made with the stripes running horizontally, which I find very pleasing – this also works well on curtains and on cushion covers. The rather lovely sash window is further adorned with some vintage china pots and glassware.
OPPOSITE This London drawing room has simple scrubbed floorboards and a magnificent sash window that opens out onto the garden. The depth of the skirting boards/baseboards gives a clue as to the age of the property. We furnished the room with a wooden sofa and a selection of cheery cushions in Jolly Stripe and Hatley, both printed in charcoal on natural linen.

Decorative Details

Having been a stylist for the past 50 or so years, I am always arranging vignettes at home – little cameos of the life of a collector. These are usually colour co-ordinated and are made to evoke a particular mood. They are not always practical to live with, but they are very useful for making beautiful photographs. In a house with open fires, dusting so many objects could easily become a full-time occupation, but I accept the dust of everyday life and deal with it when the mood takes me. It is often on days when I am cleaning the beloved objects that I decide to rearrange them.

After a change of wallpaper, paint, curtains or furnishings, great joy can be had in hunting for different paraphernalia, furniture and decorations for your newly decorated room. My current obsession is Staffordshire figurines, particularly the large black and white ones. I find them mildly comical and slightly creepy, but also very beautiful. There is something comforting about offering a home to an object with no discernible use, other than being a whimsical ornament to fill an empty shelf. Over time, you can assemble a collection of similar statues to make a playful statement. Black- or gilt-framed prints, readily found at antique markets, will complement the earthy monotones of charcoal fabrics and enhance the space beautifully.

Scouring markets and vintage shops is an immensely satisfying pastime. Often a single object can be the starting point for a whole series of decorating decisions that determine the character of a room. I recall the excitement of finding a set of black and white decorative plates, which are relatively rare. I gave them a wall of their own in my all-white kitchen, where they make a lovely monochrome display.

RIGHT This windowsill at Brook Cottage is furnished with black and white artefacts, including Staffordshire figurines, family photographs and a bird cage. The set of plates on the adjacent wall was found in an antique shop in Sussex.

"After a change of wallpaper, great joy can be had in hunting for paraphernalia for your newly decorated room."

Of course, you can introduce any colour at all into a scheme, but I find that the calming effect of a restricted colour palette makes for a peaceful space, which especially appeals to me at the moment.

Since writing my book *Green Housekeeping*, in which I extolled the virtue of furnishing your rooms with vintage artefacts rather than new, I can honestly say that I have introduced almost nothing into my home that has not had a past life before it came into my possession. My point is that there are enough objects already existing in the world that we surely do not need vast factories to churn out more cheap goods that are not made to last and are sure to end their lives in a landfill site, where they will remain for millennia to come.

OPPOSITE AND RIGHT In this bedroom/bathroom in a Georgian former priory in Somerset, a zinc-topped table is furnished with luxurious scented candles and black soap on vintage black and white saucers. These lovely accessories complement the charcoal Hatley wallpaper and French Toile curtains, and play a major part in bringing the room to life. The carved wooden tie-backs have been painted gloss black. ABOVE All the walls in Atlanta Bartlett's house in Kent are clad with whitewashed pine panelling. Here she has created a display of vintage antlers.

"I love to combine old and new, useful and not, but all somehow fitting the situation perfectly."

New things have a place, but they must be as ethically made as possible, they must be designed with longevity in mind, and they must have a beauty and a function that will last.

The loveliness of our Tulips & Roses fabric comes into its own when coloured in gentle shades of charcoal grey. When paired with simple, black-toned accessories, its floral extravagance is tempered by the stark black of the furniture and decorative pieces. Black-framed prints and Staffordshire pieces add interest to the scene. Even a pile of unread and most probably unreadable books, beautifully and anciently bound, has its own character. I love to combine old and new, useful and not, but all somehow fitting the situation perfectly.

The more sparse the decoration of a room, the more important the artefacts it contains. A single chair, pot or picture can have a dramatic effect. This looks wonderful in photographs, in which simplicity can be as dramatic and theatrical as a room filled with treasures. It can also work very well in real life, especially in houses (both old and new) that have excellent architectural credentials and spacious interiors. In my home, there is only one room that suits this aesthetic: the laundry (see page 57). It looks beautiful furnished with a pair of chippy white painted chairs and a single bowl, with a Roman blind/shade in plain linen. In real life, there are always at least two baskets of laundry resting on those chairs. But the room works, in its clean empty way.

LEFT The third print in our collection, New Penny, began life as a pale pink ditsy design on white cotton. Here it is seen in its newest incarnation, in shades of charcoal printed onto natural linen. These handsome curtains have been lined and interlined and were designed to reach down to the floor with an additional 2cm/¾in in length to create this puddled effect. Floor-length curtains always bring a magnificent sense of grandeur to a room. BELOW Provence Toile is an inverted version of French Toile, with natural linen as the predominant colour. Both designs are based on a tattered old lampshade I bought in France many years ago, which had a lovely print in a beautiful cherry red and white. It was kept in storage for several years before we redrew the sprigged florals and created two lovely fabrics.

I was once visited by an interior decorator and designer, who was overwhelmed by the vast quantity of "stuff" in my house. Having promised me that she would put everything back in its place afterwards, she proceeded to empty my kitchen of all the decorative but well-used and much-loved objects that furnish my many shelves. It was an aesthetic experiment that was intended to show me the beauty of minimalism in interiors.

Now, I am not, in any shape or form, a minimalist. However, I was curious to find out if this clever and well-known designer was right, and to see whether my kitchen would hold its own when stripped of any sort of adornment. I soon discovered that it did not. Without its "stuff", the kitchen became a sad, bare, low-ceilinged room, large and empty of not only things, but of life and soul, warmth and charm. The designer did not bring anything back into the room, as she had promised she would, instead leaving me to fetch all the items that she had placed outside and carry them inside again.

That was my house, a small cottage, with small windows and, despite being a listed building, with few architectural features that can carry it without embellishment from its owners. Minimalism has almost no place here at Brook Cottage, as the designer's experiment revealed. However, the right room, furnished with only a few carefully curated artefacts and the right fabric, can be a thing of startling beauty.

OPPOSITE The grand and glorious Tulips & Roses is shown here printed in varying shades of charcoal and grey. The beautifully drawn roses with their exquisite details have a grandeur when made into generous, full-length curtains, which are a focal point of this room. Although the black-painted furniture looks very fine here, a different accent colour (such as red lacquer or gentle pink) would also work well in this setting. RIGHT Old paintings adorn the walls of this candlelit book room. Vintage books, or indeed any books, are the most hospitable furnishing a room can ever have and always lend a congenial atmosphere, whether they are read or not. If you would like to start your own collection, auction houses and second-hand shops are excellent sources for filling your empty shelves.

ABOVE LEFT The objects on this windowsill make a charming ensemble, even though there seems no rhyme nor reason for them to go together. The crumbling books are purely decorative and are held together with string. ABOVE RIGHT A collection of creamware jugs in varying shades of white. OPPOSITE A vintage road-works light has found a new purpose as a floor lamp. The curtain fabric is Hatley in charcoal printed onto white linen.

OVERLEAF LEFT A curtain in paisley-inspired New Penny in charcoal on white is lined with the tiny Metro print, in which fine lines are interspersed with floral sprigs. Together they make a lovely contrasting pair. Black and zinc accessories give an edge to the soft florals. RIGHT A bedroom table, covered with a striped cloth, serves as a desk. The curtains are made from Hatley and the cushions from Meggernie and Paris Rose, all in charcoal.

Curtains and Drapes

If you want to ensure privacy or block out an unsightly view, you will need to think carefully about how to dress your windows so as to allow light in but still have a screening effect. Whether your home is blessed with beautiful Georgian casements, tiny windows or great expanses of modern glass, a charcoal print can be a most gratifying choice for curtains or blinds/shades.

I am often perplexed as to why certain colours work in a given room and others simply do not, and I think it very much depends on what is going on outside the window as well as how the space is used by its inhabitants. Above all, you also need to consider the climate before you decide on a colour palette for your interior. Here in England, the weather can be bleak or bright, damp or dry, so the quality of the light is a key consideration. Harsh light can have a very different effect to cloudy weather, and a south-facing room will have a very different light to one that faces north. Just as with paint colours, you need to view your prospective fabrics at all times of the day to gauge how light affects their appearance.

I advocate generosity in curtains – they should be as full and as long as possible, whatever the room and however it is decorated. When hanging floor-length curtains, make sure their length exceeds the height of the rail by about 2cm/¾in, allowing the fabric to puddle on the floor rather than floating above it. Interlining is a must for better insulation and using a patterned lining instead of plain will bring an extra dimension, though printed fabrics will fade over time if exposed to bright sunlight. This must be considered when choosing the lining, unless you are planning to install additional blinds/shades, cotton voile curtains or simple louvred shutters. These can be very useful, but will always be secondary to the main curtains.

OPPOSITE This is the grand staircase hall at the Priory, the Georgian house in Somerset belonging to my daughter Kate Howells and her husband Christopher. The complicated curtains were made remotely by our amazing friend Maria Checkley, who worked only with a scribbled drawing, vague measurements and a debatable knowledge of geometry from her clients on the ground. The fabric used is India Rose, an elegant vertical stripe, with matching cushions on the window seat.

OVERLEAF LEFT This is an entirely different staircase, situated in our office in London's Chelsea, which we left in 2018. Here, we opted for a Roman blind/shade made from Hatley in charcoal, which worked well with the black-painted woodwork and the whitewashed walls. RIGHT Full-length curtains in Meggernie on white linen. FAR RIGHT A now-discontinued fabric design in a study with beautiful sash windows.

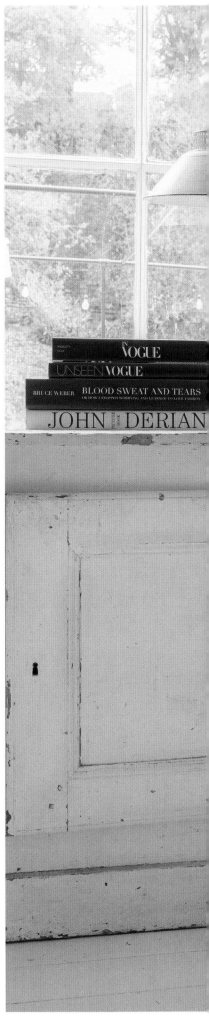

LEFT, ABOVE AND OPPOSITE Here we see three very different designs in charcoal. On the left is Alderney, an elegant floral with beautiful shading in various shades of grey. The middle image is Toile de Poulet, inspired by a rather lumpy original and redrawn by me as a fine and delicate toile. On the right is India Rose, featuring beautiful oriental florals placed in vertical stripes.

ABOVE LEFT Elgin, a pared-back reinterpretation of an Indian motif from 1764, has been newly coloured in shades of grey. ABOVE RIGHT The Julia print was designed as a secondary fabric and is used mostly for linings. Here the pretty design, in charcoal, is given the limelight as a main fabric for a curtain. The delicate shading on the floral posies is rather fetching when paired with deep black painted furniture. OPPOSITE Our Constance design began life as a multi-coloured print and is seen here in monochrome charcoal. The colour scheme is calm and muted, yet there are plenty of details to amuse the eye. The books, more than 100 years old, have been given a new occupation as a thing of curious beauty.

Common Thread: Linen

At the time of writing, all our designs are printed onto a base of pure linen. It is the most ecologically sound fabric available, for many reasons. Linen is made from flax, one of the few textile fibres that grows well in northern Europe, Belgium and Ireland being two major players – though we have recently begun using linen woven here in the UK. Flax thrives in poor soil and requires little water and no pesticides, herbicides or fertilizers. It can be used to produce not just linen fibre but flax seeds and flaxseed oil, so nothing is wasted.

Apart from its innate beauty, linen has the ability to keep you cool because of the fibres' hollow core. This is what makes it such an appealing material for bed linen as well as clothing. It also has hypoallergenic and anti-inflammatory properties. The only drawback is that the harvesting is mostly done by hand and involves leaving the pulled flax plants to rot for several weeks to make it easier to extract the fibres. Many stages of linen production require human beings, unlike cotton, which tends to be produced by machine. This is why the price difference between cotton and linen is so great.

OPPOSITE LEFT Plain, unadorned linen has an extraordinary beauty and character. The curtain here is made from newly woven cloth, while the chair is upholstered in antique linen with a cerise Hatley cushion. **RIGHT** Vintage tureens blend in with this fitted tablecloth, which was made by Maria Checkley from washed ivory linen. The embroidered napkins bring in accents of red.

The colour and texture of our linen fabric depend on the harvest of the flax, the dampness of the weather and the amount of sunshine during its growth and harvest. For this reason, we always recommend looking at a swatch before making a big purchase of fabric so that you can check the precise colour of that particular batch.

Studying the origins of linen, I discovered that it first made its appearance in around 8000 BC. There is evidence that linen fibre was used to make nets and twine, remnants having been found beside several lakes in Switzerland. Its resilience and hard-wearing properties have therefore lasted more than 10,000 years.

The ancient Egyptians may have used linen as a form of currency, and nowadays there is a thriving market for 18th- and 19th-century French linen sheets. On a recent buying trip, Kate and I purchased a number of these sheets, including some that had been exquisitely hand-embroidered with their owners' initials.

In the early days of Cabbages & Roses, we used to stock many of these sheets, which we had printed with our designs. It was difficult to keep up with demand, so they were slowly phased out, but we have recently decided to reintroduce them. Each one will be screen-printed by hand, adding even more value to the heavy woven linen pieces – our very own currency.

PREVIOUS PAGES A view through to my bedroom from the sitting room of my London apartment. The fabric, Toile de Poulet, was chosen to complement the wonderful natural aged wood of the shutter doors, of which there are three pairs in this tiny space. A free-standing bath, just out of sight to the left of the bed, made this a luxurious home until we left for Somerset in 2018.

LEFT A mellow pastoral scene with plain linen curtains at the Georgian windows of the Priory. BELOW This picture was taken in our Langton Street shop to promote our handmade soap. OPPOSITE The laundry at Brook Cottage has a Roman blind/shade made from an antique sheet found in a French market. The chippy painted chairs have starred in many a photograph over the years.

CABBAGES & ROSES

OPPOSITE, THIS PAGE AND OVERLEAF This chair, photographed in a house in London's New Cross, was bought from Appley Hoare. Our range of linen accessories was photographed at the same house, which at the time belonged to Atlanta Bartlett. The location was chosen for its architectural details and light-filled rooms, including its heavenly bedroom.

Hues of Blue

AQUA, BLUE, DOVE, FRENCH BLUE, LILAC AND NAVY

Shades of blue are inestimably varied, from cool, icy hues to warm violets. When we consider the psychology of colour, blue is often associated with feelings of calm and serenity, representing all that is secure and orderly.

We have had to divide this colourway into several different categories, as it proved impossible to fix upon just one version. Our main blue is the colour of a good sky, while French blue has tones of grey and teal has an element of green mixed in. Navy is the right side of dark and dove is barely there, but enough to make a quiet statement.

Following on from the blues is aqua, a soft sage hue that floats between blue and silvery green. I would love to produce a floral print in green one day; for now, aqua is as close as we get. When printed onto a natural linen base, this pastoral shade is beautifully understated. Lilac is a warmer shade, with hints of violet, but still serene and soothing.

Layering: Playing with Scale

Small secondary prints always enhance an interiors scheme and using them in the same colourway as the main pattern will help to break up the landscape. Patterns such as Metro, a fine stripe that features tiny, delicate floral sprigs, and Scoopy, an all-over dot, work well with large and small designs alike. French Toile has been my choice for kitchen curtains and blinds/shades for the past 15 years, teamed with cushions in a mix of these two small-scale designs.

In a sitting room, too, there is always scope to introduce a secondary or tertiary print. Our linen fabrics are suitable for upholstery, albeit for light use only. Amazingly, my sofa has an 18-year-old slip cover made from our linen, which still shows no sign of wear and tear.

Bedroom schemes present a wonderful opportunity to mix and match. Curtains and their linings, interior blinds/shades, table coverings, quilts, cushions, and last but not least bed valances. Co-ordinating in colour but not scale, a bed valance is the perfect finishing touch. This is where a small print can come into its own.

The colour that we call dove is a whisper of grey-blue and in the Hatley design it makes a wonderful duvet cover. The combination of white walls with a pattern of scattered rosy blooms suggests a simple, peaceful life. Linen will naturally crease and I believe it only gathers more beauty and charm the more crumpled it becomes.

Wallpapers in shades of blue have an instantly soothing effect that is smart, restful and reassuring. Blending into the background but suggesting a subtle elegance, Paris Rose works with any style of decor, from modern through to traditional. The design is printed onto a non-woven base rather than paper, which gives the wallpaper a lovely texture. It is made using a technique called flexographic printing, which was invented in the 1890s and is perfect for intricately drawn patterns such as Paris Rose.

The machine used in the production of our flexo-printed wallpapers is more than 100 years old. It uses rollers with designs elevated above the surface – similar to a finely engraved rubber stamp. Engraving a roller is an expensive process, so designs need to be chosen carefully in order to get the most use out of them, but a single roller can be used to print the same design in several different colourways. The Hatley wallpaper was another obvious choice to be printed using this method and is available in a variety of colours and backgrounds. At the opposite end of the spectrum is Catherine Rose, a ditzy floral in which the flowers are neatly dispersed across the background. Pretty and fresh, it is ideal for a bathroom or nursery and has a beautiful chalky texture.

Although our patterns may seem tailor-made for country living, many of our customers are city dwellers, who use our gentle floral fabric and wallpaper designs to bring a little of this pastoral fantasy into their homes. Monochrome patterns, even those featuring a flourish of flowers, have a suavity and chicness that is well suited to urban interiors. As we saw in the previous chapter, choosing a stripe to co-ordinate with a floral in a similar colour is a failsafe choice. The stripe will help to ground a mostly floral decorating scheme and is sure to add an air of sophistication. You can also combine the sparsity of our Hatley print with plain, unprinted linens and natural sisal floor matting to evoke a gentle minimalism that works in all settings – city, seaside or country – particularly in hues of blue.

PAGE 62 A Constance cushion in French blue, a shade mixed with grey and teal.

PAGES 64-65 A collage showing the full spectrum of blues in our collections.

PREVIOUS PAGES Hatley in dove is a wonderful choice for bed linen.

OPPOSITE A curtain in navy Elgin with subtle tones of grey is a handsome foil for antique prints in black and gold frames. ABOVE LEFT French Toile and Provence Toile work beautifully together in soft blue and buff tones with a bedcover in Mary, a gently faded floral design. ABOVE RIGHT A cushion made from Ditzy in dove on a white linen base cloth.

CABBAGES & ROSES

"Wallpapers in shades of blue have an instantly soothing effect that is smart, restful and reassuring."

OPPOSITE ABOVE AND BELOW Cushions are the finishing touch, a homely addition to a room providing comfort and colour. Easily changeable from room to room, and in varying shapes and sizes. The monotone grey-blues printed onto a soft buff linen work well with masculine stripes, taking the edge off the floral femininity. LEFT Hatley wallpaper brings warmth to this stone-floored entrance hall. The chippy painted chairs with their small Jolly Stripe cushions add further colour and texture, preventing the space from feeling cold.

Decorative Details

Our French blue fabrics have an air of peacefulness, as the designs are subtly drawn with grey undertones that fade elegantly into the background. Unassuming in their character, they are a natural choice for every room in the home. A simple cushion covered in our India Rose fabric in this colourway, placed on a plain ivory linen-upholstered armchair, is a beautiful sight all on its own. Alternatively, cover a round table with a custom-made floor-length tablecloth interlined with an old blanket. Placed in an entrance hall or tucked into the corner of a drawing room or bedroom, this will serve as a beautiful surface on which to arrange a collection of glass and silverware, worn galvanized metal objects or piles of books. A display of this kind should be a reflection of your own personality, with the cloth providing the starting point.

White flowers and silver leaves will complement the freshness of aqua, though its muted tones will be enhanced by any plant-based decoration. The floral designer Constance Spry once wrote that "there are scoffers who find truly comic eccentricity in the consideration of beauty in what they call common vegetables". However, I am not one of them. During the winter months, when flowers are sparse, I find that fruit and vegetables can be a valuable source of greenery. Consider displaying a bowl of artichokes or a vase of curly kale or wild blackcurrant sprigs in your kitchen.

Nothing in our photographs is perfect, except where the colours are just right in the printed fabric, or in the freshly picked flowers. The reality is worn and faded cushion covers, a wonky lampshade, slightly haphazard styling – this is who we are, a mixture of the excellent and the slightly "off". We make a great effort here and there to deflect attention from what is not at its best. A loved object will always find a place, and if our aspirations dictate that something past its best must be disposed of, perhaps they need to be reassessed.

OPPOSITE India Rose makes for an unassuming yet elegant table. Alderney in a matching blue dresses the windows. RIGHT An armchair upholstered in Mary.

OVERLEAF Metal lamp bases and other silver-toned accessories complement a tablecloth in Hatley and a curtain in Elgin.

Curtains and Drapes

As with all our fabrics, the difference between a blue pattern on a ground of natural buff-coloured linen and the same hue on a pure white ground is immense. Print one of our designs onto a natural linen base and it takes on a decorous air, demanding interlining, lining and fine workmanship in the making of curtains, slip covers or cushions. When printed on white, however, the very same design becomes fresh and vibrant.

Blue and white is a combination ideally suited to coastal settings. I envisage a gleaming white beach hut with a white linen curtain made from any one of our blue-patterned fabrics gently blowing in the wind – unlined and unsewn, washed and bleached by the salty air and sea breezes. That is the beauty of fabric; it wields great power in dictating how and where it should be used.

Our blue-and-white fabrics are deliciously light, with delicate designs both striped and floral, which have an air of serenity and quietude. The mellow tones of blue and French blue are particularly suited to an all-white environment, particularly in hot countries, where all you need is a cool breeze and shade from the sun.

Generosity in curtains is an important investment in any decorating scheme. After all, curtains are an expensive outlay and need to be considered carefully. I have always advocated getting the very best curtains you can afford and I believe you absolutely must not skimp on either the quality or quantity of the fabric. If it means delaying the completion of a room in order to save up for the perfect window treatment, you will be thankful in the end that you decided to wait. To have to live with second best, when such an investment is required, will be disheartening for a very long time.

Whatever the room, interlining your curtains will add to the grandeur and warmth they provide. A co-ordinating lining in a smaller print will add visual interest as part of a layered interiors scheme. Curtain headings are a matter of personal choice, there is no right or wrong. However, personally I like the simplest of headings, as my ceilings are low and cannot take anything grander than a simple gathered top. A decorative braid at the edge of a curtain adds interest and is a relatively cheap addition for the impact it creates.

PREVIOUS PAGES LEFT Constance fabric sits harmoniously in a calm and interesting scheme of blues, black and silver. The curtain is made from Alderney, similar in colour but a completely different design. RIGHT Black candlesticks add a contemporary twist to this dining table. Subdued greys and Toile de Poulet curtains add an element of calm in an otherwise deliciously crowded scene.

OPPOSITE LEFT Delicate Metro in aqua on pure buff-coloured linen. RIGHT This restful version of Provence Toile sits quietly and beautifully alongside a set of black-framed prints and an old Swedish chest with peeling grey paint.

OPPOSITE These photographs show how the same scene can be subtly transformed by a different choice of curtain fabric. Here, our Mary design works beautifully with the black and buff accessories, which give substance to the light and faded tones of the blue and stone-coloured print. Mary's full-blown roses have a faded grandeur and a large repeat that would work well in an elegant drawing room. RIGHT Constance in the teal colourway is bolder yet more feminine, the images more defined and finely drawn. I think it would be more suitable for a bedroom. The accessories have a similar strengthening effect.

"Whichever Cabbages & Roses fabric you choose for your curtains, you will discover that they all have a peculiarly English beauty."

Cabbages & Roses offers a selection of handmade trims: cotton braids, bobbles and fan edging in colours that we have selected to co-ordinate with the colours of our fabrics. A pelmet/valance edged in braid, together with a matching trim on the leading edge of the curtain, will make a beautiful statement, especially if you select a trim that will highlight the main colour of the curtain fabric.

My preference has always been to hang curtains from poles, mainly because they seem to be the simplest and most elegant solution. There are many options available, from the simplest wooden poles with understated finials to beautiful, intricately carved designs that will make more of a statement. You also have a choice of materials,

including painted or varnished wood, or perhaps an old brass pole. It is worth the effort to find a design that suits you and the room. A pole is the most straightforward option, but there are a multitude of alternatives, not least a beautifully designed pelmet/valance that will conceal the curtain heading. The only curtain hanging method I cannot tolerate is the visible plastic track – but even this is fine if it is hidden behind a pelmet/valance in this way.

Had impecuniosity not been the lingering hinderance in my life, I would perhaps have opted for bespoke pelmets/valances, adorned with trims and specially designed for each room of my house. If you have the right contacts and know a skilled maker who can bring your vision to life, this would be a lovely option, especially now that excess seems to be overtaking minimalism as the preferred aesthetic in the home. Pelmets/valances will look best in rooms that have a generous ceiling height, which will show off the loveliness that a pelmet can contribute to a room.

Whichever Cabbages & Roses fabric you choose for your curtains, you will discover that they all have a peculiarly English beauty. Within the vast decorative fabric market, I have always been drawn to the subtle and delicate. There is an element of quiet in all our designs, so that adaptability and ease of change is inherent within them. Curtains in particular will be an expensive commitment, so it is crucial that your choice is something you are prepared to live with for a long time. Fashion fads and trendy fabric choices may limit the ancillary changes you are able to make at a later date, whereas a timeless and versatile design will offer longevity and lasting pleasure for years or even decades to come.

PREVIOUS PAGES Curtains in teal French Toile and aqua Toile de Poulet.

OPPOSITE The feminine Charlotte design on white linen makes a light and airy window treatment that would suit a bedroom or bathroom.
ABOVE RIGHT AND RIGHT Either the faded Ditzy print or Catherine Rose in the same shade of blue would make a refreshing choice for a set of kitchen curtains.

ABOVE LEFT AND RIGHT The dove colourway is a soft, faded grey, which makes a delicate statement and can slip unobtrusively into any decorating scheme. It is seen here in Hatley with a charming lining in the Julia design. The faint fragility of Hatley gives it a nostalgic poignancy and the mixing of motifs – with a lining that is busier than the main fabric – adds another dimension to the curtains. Used as a main curtain or perhaps a summer tablecloth, the combination of these two designs is a perfect pairing.
OPPOSITE Full-length, generously pooled curtains are always my preferred choice, especially when lined and interlined for a luxurious weightiness. These are made from the beautiful Alderney design in dove. The sprawling pattern of flowers, stems and leaves is elegant yet light-hearted and can be accessorized with both contemporary and traditional pieces.

Common Thread: Painterly Prints

Throughout history, the wish to adorn bodies and interiors with beautiful fabric has inspired the decorative art of textile design. Until the first half of the 20th century, cloth had enormous social significance. Even nowadays, different garments and furnishings are often similar in their design and construction, so the quality of the fabric serves as an unmistakable marker of luxury and status.

There are some textiles that cost many hundreds of pounds or dollars a metre/yard, usually because they are printed by hand or because they have an intricate design that uses many hand-mixed colours. Others are produced on a large scale to make them affordable to the masses. Cabbages & Roses fabrics, some of which are still hand printed, find themselves somewhere in the middle of the market. The fact that we design and produce them ourselves makes them a special and unique investment. In order to reduce waste, all our fabrics are printed to order, so no stock is left languishing in a warehouse. Any fabric remnants are made into products – even our clothing offcuts are put to good use.

In addition to our monochrome fabrics, our range also includes a number of multi-coloured designs. The joy of the multicoloured is the unbridled extravagance with which you can accessorize. When you have so many colours to work with, any one of them can be picked out – or you can highlight all of them with a vibrant bouquet of flowers. When we convert multicoloured prints into monotone versions, the blues are often the most entrancing – they have a huge variety of personalities, which change with each new shade.

RIGHT Beautiful and delicate, Toile de Poulet in French blue on natural linen is a perfect foil for Swedish antique grey furniture and black- and zinc-coloured accessories. The gilt-framed prints add uplifting colour. OPPOSITE Dark blue Elgin fabric adorns the panel behind the bed and some of the window seat and bed cushions. The Jolly Stripe cushions in navy have a grounding effect.

In the tradition of Cabbages & Roses, most of our blue patterns bear the hallmark of gentle fadedness, whereas others carry the strength of deep navy. One example is the elegant Elgin design – a pared-back reinterpretation of a hand-painted Indian motif dating back to 1764. This print is available in several colourways, each taking on a personality of its own. When its neutral pale grey sub-tones are mixed with deep navy blue, this combination of the bold and the delicate makes it exactly right for a chic drawing room.

A completely different design is Mary in French blue on a base of natural-coloured linen. This handsome fabric features overblown pale blue roses strewn across the cloth and barely-there leaves floating in the background. With a large repeat, it is a grand statement piece and fits as well into a stately room as a high-ceilinged farmhouse. It is warm, grand and elegant without self-importance. We have also trialled this print on thick, luxurious, hand-woven linen from Belgium, with exquisite results.

The teal fabrics are an elegant alternative to their French blue cousins. This unusual shade incorporates touches of turquoise, green and dark blue to form an exquisite sea green mixed with sea blue. This colourway highlights our beautifully drawn florals more than any other. One of the loveliest is Constance, which is made in the teal colourway as well as French blue, both on natural linen. As I write, I am imagining a four-poster bed dressed with teal Constance, lined with either New Penny or finely striped Metro in the same hue. Perhaps our next book will feature this exact bed – I do hope so.

LEFT A selection of antique linen sheets, found in French markets, have recently been printed with our designs. Each one is unique and has its own inherent beauty. Although expensive to buy and hand print, they can make wonderful curtains, especially when found in pairs. In some cases they can even be hung on clip rings without the need for any sewing. The sturdier sheets can be used for upholstery or slip covers, while the lighter weights are better suited to tablecloths or bedcovers.

BELOW During lockdown/stay-at-home, when antique markets were cancelled, we discovered that printing onto new heavy Belgian linen produced similar results. Its uneven weave adds so much character. Here we have printed Mary in blue – the beautiful roses are enhanced and enriched by the soft, crumpled texture of the fabric.

"Most of our blue patterns bear the hallmark of gentle fadedness, whereas others carry the strength of deep navy."

PREVIOUS PAGES Paris Rose wallpaper adorns this elegant window wall. The subtle blue tones, printed on a buff-coloured ground, bring restful comfort to the high-ceilinged room. The pattern does not overwhelm in the summer but makes for a cozy room in the winter. The old French armchairs are furnished with cushions in similar hues to the wallpaper. The design on the left is India Rose, an eastern-inspired print laid out in vertical lines, and on the right is Constance in shades of grey and blue.

LEFT Paris Rose on natural linen makes a charming set of curtains for this light-filled study with its old painted table. The gentle floral print is a versatile design that does not intrude or shout – it is an elegant and accepting friend. The rug adds a touch of warmth and picks up the grey-blue of the fabric.

OPPOSITE These rolls of wallpaper are waiting to be hung. The design is Mary in lilac and the scale of the pattern requires it to be printed on extra-wide paper. In bold lilacs and mauves with sage-green leaves, it is at its best when hung in a large room to show off its full glory. Neither contemporary nor traditional, it is spectacular and unexpected, and looks lovely when teamed with plain linen and as many lilac flowers as possible. RIGHT Floral displays enhance any interiors scheme, especially when they are dramatic in scale. Here a mighty bunch of buddleia has been installed in a giant ancient zinc vat, making a magnificent show. When the flowers fade, they can be replaced in the winter months with dried twigs adorned with twinkling lights. White linen curtains are a calm and neutral foil for the extravagant walls. They are also impressive in themselves, thanks to the scale and generosity of their undulating width.

Lilac Love

Just as gentle and subdued as blues are all things lilac – that colour that lies somewhere between violet and dusty blue. It may not be a shade that immediately springs to mind when you are selecting furnishings for a room, but it is a colour that should not be ignored. It is a restful shade, just like our blues, but a little warmer in tone, especially when it is used with the right greens and greys.

Lilac or purple has always been known as a regal colour, perhaps because for much of human history it was so prohibitively expensive to produce. It was not until the 1850s, when a synthetic dye was invented, that purple fabrics became more widely available. Before this, only the very wealthy, such as kings and queens, were able to afford textiles dyed with Tyrian purple. It is thought that this natural pigment was first produced by the Phoenicians more than 3,500 years ago in what is now known as Lebanon.

To make even a small amount of this incredibly valuable dye, you would first have to harvest around 250,000 molluscs from a species called Bolinus brandaris. These had to be individually cracked so that the purple mucus contained within could be extracted and left to dry for a precise amount of time to produce just one ounce of usable dye. The result was a long-lasting and vibrant shade of purple. Luckily for the poor molluscs, once the synthetic version was invented, their working days were numbered.

Lilac remains one of my favourite colours in our palette of fabric and wallpaper designs. A particularly memorable example is the Mary lilac wallpaper, which my daughter Kate chose for the walls of her dining room. It was a difficult room to decorate because it was so spectacular in scale that it needed something dramatic, yet not too overwhelming, to do it justice. It is also something of a thoroughfare. This does not seem to cause much of a problem, although Kate has plans for this room to double as a library, and too much through traffic is not conducive to a quiet read.

Where you have a dramatic wall covering, it is as well to have simple curtains. Here, Kate has used a beautiful Belgian linen in the colour of light ivory. Cabbages & Roses usually stocks this particular linen, though at the moment of writing, supply is difficult due to the pandemic and other factors such as a poor harvest. However, we do still have lovely white linen, which is available either printed or plain, and soon we shall have a stock of antique linen sheets that can serve as instant ready-made curtains.

The extravagant tablecloth has been custom-made to fit the table exactly, again in plain white linen. Its gathered skirt was designed to make sitting at the table more comfortable, because a straight overhang can sometimes be difficult to arrange neatly over knees. The same crisp white linen has been used to make simple yet elegant slip covers for a set of folding garden chairs – a marvellously affordable alternative to proper dining chairs.

LEFT Mary wallpaper in lilac and sage green graces the walls of this magnificent dining room. Its large-scale floral extravaganza demands too much attention for there to be a competing fabric anywhere else in the room. Instead, Maria Checkley used plain ivory linen to make the curtains, frilled tablecloth and chair covers. The antique French ceramic tureens complement the scheme perfectly.

"Lilac may not be a shade that immediately springs to mind when you are selecting furnishings for a room, but it is a colour that should not be ignored."

The wonderful thing about a lilac room is the array of flowers that can be brought in to enhance the space from spring through to late summer: white and purple lilac, buddleia and silver-leaved lavender. Indeed, anything with silver leaves is magnificent in such a large room. Its scale demands huge arrangements, but I find that gigantic floral displays can work even in a room with lesser proportions; boldness always has a place. In Kate's dining room, the vast galvanized pots detract from the genteel prettiness – a touch of masculinity in contrast with the feminine wallpaper.

Surprisingly, or not, I love black-framed pictures in a lilac-themed room, hung in sets or in pairs. Black frames bring weight and sophistication, but gilt frames also work very well. A gilt-framed mirror has since been purchased for this room – I expect it shall appear one day in photographic form. Another surprising co-ordinate for lilac is lacquer red, and it is my ambition one day to incorporate both colours in a scheme.

Most of our floral tones have been inspired by nature, none more so than our lilac colourway. A glorious lilac tablecloth, in the Hatley design, was an absolute joy to style, with the hostas offering up their short-lived flowers just in time for our photography (see pages 150-151). Not to mention the divine sweet peas and lavender – seen against lush greenery on the walls of Brook Cottage, they demonstrated just how well lilac and green work together.

ABOVE The gentle floral medallions of our Julia print make the lining of this charming white linen curtain. The main fabric is Charlotte, a beautifully drawn design consisting of posies of flowers. A lilac Hatley duvet cover adds to this restful bedroom, which is brightened by the sharp green and gentle white of the flowers. A balance of colours is the key to an inviting, interesting room.
OPPOSITE The back wall of our beautiful shop in Bruton, Somerset, is covered in lilac Mary wallpaper. This space, once a car repair workshop, has been transformed by the extravagantly feminine pattern, the ornate gilt-framed mirror and the charmingly chippy old iron bed. The bed is dressed with lilac Hatley bed linen and a cushion in pink Tulips & Roses.

La Vie en Rose

BERRY RED, BLOSSOM, CERISE, PINK, ROSE AND RASPBERRY

Without a doubt, pink and red are our best-selling colourways by far. Hatley in cerise has sold the most metres of fabric, but anything in pink is close behind. Though cerise is a relatively simple colour to get right, pink is an entirely different matter.

Pink conjures up romantic charm in a sweet spectrum from bright fuchsia to pale rose, yet it is the most difficult colour to work with. Moreover, the same pink will react very differently depending on the base cloth it is printed on. It has taken years to perfect our pinks and reds, but eventually we fixed upon several shades for our collections.

Raspberry and berry red are warm colours that make for a cozy atmosphere. Elgin, an Indian-inspired print with deep red accents in the raspberry colourway, would look completely at home in either a grand drawing room or a small study. The same pattern looks very different in pink, a shade that highlights the finely drawn floral motif.

ALAMINE® 230

SULKING ROOM
PINK® 295

ANCY'S
USHES® 278

CINDER ROSE™ 246

D EARTH™ 64

RANGWALI® 296

CTURE
ALLERY RED® 42

PINK GROUND® 202

CARNADINE™ 248

SETTING
PLASTER® 231

Exquisite

ALWAYS KEEP Y
BEAUTIFUL IMAGI
& EXQUISITE H

CABBAGES & ROSES

ES & ROSE   ABBAG   ES

CABBAGES & ROSES   CABBAGES

ROSES   CABBAGES & ROSES   CABBAG

CABBAGES & ROSES
LONDON

LEONE
CANDY ORIGINALS

FINE ITALIAN
SPECIALITIES

SINCE 1857

PRODUCT OF ITALY

BBAGES & ROSE

SES   CABBA

BCE ECB EZB EKT EKP 2002

10

Layering: Pattern Density

From sparsely spaced blooms to finely drawn toiles, the colour pink has the ability to warm and brighten a space and inject personality and charm. In the hallway of Brook Cottage, I opted for an overblown printed wallpaper called Alderney in a deep raspberry pink, on an off-white ground. It transformed the forgotten and neglected staircase, lending it grandeur and a hearty dose of swagger. A large-gilt framed mirror and a simple glass-shaded ceiling light were all the adornment the brightly papered walls needed. The curtain, which has hung there for many a year, is a French linen sheet printed with Hatley in cerise. With its sparsely printed design, this works well as an antidote to the full-blown, all-over pattern of the walls. Hatley is a beautiful, fresh design that lifts a room's spirit. It is elegant and feminine yet never saccharine – and in cerise, it is strikingly sturdy. As well as furnishing fabrics, cerise Hatley has adorned many clothing designs, from pyjamas to dresses. It is a guaranteed sell-out, every time.

PAGE 102 The curtains in my kitchen have been made in pink Tulips & Roses and trimmed with a cotton fan edge that complements the pink plates on the wall.

PREVIOUS PAGES Our pinks and reds cover the full spectrum, from soft and romantic to bold and rich.

ABOVE Jolly Stripe curtains with a cushion in Elgin. OPPOSITE This delicious pile of new and vintage cushions includes three of our prints: Paris Rose, Three-Inch Stripe and Toile de Poulet, all in raspberry.

PREVIOUS PAGES For many years, the staircase hall at Brook Cottage was rather neglected, but it has recently been papered in our Alderney print in raspberry. I have teamed the new wallpaper with an old curtain, which was made years ago from an antique linen sheet printed with Hatley in cerise. The paint on the wall and woodwork is Hardwick White by Farrow & Ball.

RIGHT On a shelf in my bathroom, a jug of pink flowers echoes the Catherine Rose wallpaper behind. BELOW RIGHT AND OPPOSITE This tablecloth was once a linen sheet, woven on a narrow loom many years ago and stitched together. It has been hand-printed in pink Podge, a design named after our favourite printer. The pillow on the bed is printed with Alderney in raspberry.

To warm the staircase further, I painted the woodwork a grey-blue shade from Farrow & Ball, which is exactly the right tone to complement the raspberry walls. For the sake of continuity, and because I love the raspberry-coloured Alderney wallpaper so much, I also used it to paper the lavatory – possibly the smallest in England at just 53cm/21in wide. In bathrooms (and bedrooms), pink patterns work a particular magic. Whether the space is large or small, there will always be room for rosy florals to enhance walls, windows and tables. If you have a small space, I highly recommend that you go as bold as possible – it is preferable to overwhelm than underwhelm. Prints of ancestral portraits hang on the walls and yet more Staffordshire figurines decorate the top of the cistern – it never ceases to amaze me how many objects you can fit into a tiny space.

The ancient piece of linen shown here, which was woven in France on a narrow loom and sewn together with a central seam, has been hand-printed with our Podge design – a mid-sized barely-there rose with a scattering of smaller flowers. The beautiful texture of the old linen makes this a highly desirable piece. With time and good fortune, we hope to be able to find enough stock of antique linen on which to print a variety of our designs. One of the benefits of finding a pair of matching sheets is that they can make instant curtains, especially for a room in a warm climate, where there is no need to line or interline. The antithesis of Podge is the finely drawn all-over pattern of Toile de Poulet, so named because the miniature scenes it depicts are liberally scattered with chickens.

ABOVE A tattered and torn armchair bearing a cushion made from Constance linen. ABOVE RIGHT A close-up of the gently faded Ditzy printed onto white linen. RIGHT Pale pink cushions made from Catherine Rose and Three-Inch Stripe bring colour to a perfectly white bedroom. OPPOSITE TOP A vintage folding bed with striped and floral cushions. BOTTOM RIGHT Podge in pink on white linen.

The charming Catherine Rose design, featuring tiny all-over flowers in pink on a slightly off-white ground, was inspired by a fragment of fabric lining in an old work basket that I found at a market in Texas some 20 years ago. We put the pattern into repeat and, since then, many thousands of metres have been printed for both clothing and furnishing fabrics as well as wallpaper. This design has lived in my bathroom for well over 14 years and delights me still.

One of my favourite shoots was done in a beautiful townhouse in central London, in which all the huge, light-filled rooms were painted white from floor to ceiling. It was here that we photographed a family of cushions covered in Catherine Rose fabric, on a simple linen-upholstered antique bed. With minimal styling, the expanse of white was broken only by the tiny rose print, making a striking statement.

OPPOSITE A bedspread made from the Elgin print in raspberry and a large cushion in pink Provence Toile complement a cushion made from a vintage quilt. ABOVE LEFT New Penny in pink is a pretty, ditzy print that would be perfect for a child's room, a bedroom or a bathroom. ABOVE RIGHT French Toile in pink looks just right next to a display of pink lustreware china on a chippy white-painted shelf.

Decorative Details

Textures are important in a scheme and, whether textiles are printed or not, it is lovely to mix the weights and weaves to break up the potential uniformity of the furnishings. Combining antique linen grain sacks, simply woven with a single stripe, with printed fabric of the same hue will add another layer to a room. Equally, the worn, chipped patina of old shutters, a vintage painted table or a rusty bench will add variation to the overall look of an interior.

Books, too, whether grandly bound in tooled leather, or old albums whose titles have been written in ancient script, or the books you have collected over the years, are the most warming and interesting element in a room. They bring life, charm and history, wherever they come from – and are a window into the soul of the owner. After all, what could be more personal than one's choice of books? As a natural hoarder and compulsive buyer of books, I have bookshelves of some sort in every room of my house. They groan under the weight of innumerable volumes, which can also be found stacked upon tables, piled under them and by every bed in the house. I will admit to buying antique books, without having any intention of reading them, merely because I was drawn to their beautiful covers. You may detect some of them in the photographs in this book, which in turn may or may not be read.

Plates have proven to be an enchanting addition to fill an empty wall. Searching for decorative plates to add to my growing collection has become something of an obsession. Pink lustreware is a particular favourite – I have some pieces that are intricately painted, while others feature a few simple brush strokes. I don't mind if a plate is chipped or cracked and mended. In fact, I love to see a plate that has been repaired, because it has clearly been much loved in its long life.

LEFT A raspberry Paris Rose curtain is lined in a dotty print called Scoopy. Having a contrasting lining adds interest to a curtain, as it can be seen both from within the room and from outside the window. OPPOSITE LEFT The new Rosie print, a nostalgic country rose, lined with New Penny, both on natural linen. RIGHT French Toile in raspberry with accessories in deep red, gilt and black.

"Searching for decorative plates to add to my growing collection has become something of an obsession. Pink lustreware is a particular favourite – I have some pieces that are intricately painted, while others feature a few simple brush strokes."

ABOVE These napkins are made from washed and tumbled natural linen printed with our Hatley motif. The tablecloth is our Tulips & Roses design in pink, also on a natural base cloth. OPPOSITE A sofa table covered in a raspberry Hatley tablecloth with a display of framed photographs and a vintage storage box. The curtain fabric is Provence Toile in raspberry and the lampshade is made from India Rose fabric in pink.

"The worn, chipped patina of old shutters, a vintage painted table or a rusty bench will add variation to the overall look of an interior."

The lustreware cups and saucers in my collection are lovely when used together, as seen here, but somehow I like them best when separated from each other – the cups hanging prettily from the dresser/hutch, the saucers used daily.

Comfort is key in a room, especially comfortable and inviting seating in the form of sofas and armchairs. It is also important to make sure that these pieces can be easily cleaned – I always favour slip covers that can be removed and washed as needed. It is usually a good idea to wash the linen fabric before it is made into a slip cover; washing will shrink it slightly, which will make for a more sturdy cover. I also like to cover tables, especially round ones, with bespoke tablecloths that reach past floor level. These should be lined – if the cloth has no lining, simply place an old blanket underneath to give it thickness and generosity. A patterned tablecloth is a perfect foil for a display of interesting and meaningful objects that will make any room feel warm and welcoming.

If you have nothing else in a room, fresh flowers from the garden are the ultimate luxury, and easily the most wonderful thing to gift yourself on a weekly basis when they are in bloom.

OPPOSITE TOP AND BOTTOM LEFT This lovely tablecloth is made from Tulips & Roses, a multi-coloured fabric in gently faded pinks, mauves and taupe on a base of lightest grey. The much-loved bird cage has travelled with me to many a shoot. OPPOSITE RIGHT Constance in all her multi-coloured glory printed onto natural linen. RIGHT A Staffordshire figure with a curtain made from Metro in raspberry.

Common Thread: Toile

I first encountered toile de Jouy – named after the French town where these intricate pastoral prints were first produced in the 18th century – on a trip to Normandy with my family when I was just seven years old. We were staying in a beautiful little castle, and my sister and I were installed in a turret right at the top. I can still remember the glory of sleeping in a four-poster bed that was fully dressed in pink toile, with my elder sister sleeping in a matching version right next to me. It was a formative experience that I can recall vividly some 60 years later.

In a classic toile room, the same finely drawn, monotone pattern is used on the walls, ceiling, curtains, upholstery and more. Some toile rooms have walls covered in fabric rather than wallpaper. This is an expensive and time-consuming job that requires a vast amount of fabric. First, the walls need to be lined with padding. Next, the fabric panels have to be sewn together invisibly before they can be applied to the walls; sometimes the seams are covered with braid. We employed an expert to perform this tiresome task in the changing room of our Mayfair store, with the added extravagance of a tented ceiling. Heartbreakingly, when we gave up the lease, the fabric was taken down by the new owners and disposed of.

Our Toile de Poulet design was derived from a fragment of fabric that I found at a flea market in the south of France. The original pattern was rather heavily drawn with thick, uneven lines, so I re-drew the entire repeat with a fine pen – easily the most satisfying task in my life to date. Our version of the name, replacing Jouy with Poulet, came about because of the charming chickens that can be observed wandering across the print. Toile de Poulet is currently available in six colourways, but it is the deep berry red that was chosen to decorate a bedroom in my daughter's house in Somerset. It is a delightfully over-the-top scheme, in which the wallpaper, curtains and eiderdown all match.

Curtains and Drapes

Each multi-coloured print in our repertoire necessitates a number of screens to be manufactured, one for every colour in the design. When the finished fabric is made into curtains, it allows you pick out one or several of the colours in the decoration of the room. One example is Tulips & Roses, a fulsome and extravagant print featuring gently intertwined overblown roses, leaves and open tulips in gentle tones of pink and mauve on a soft grey-blue background. It would complement a display of mauve and pink china on a nearby wall. Flowers, too, can pick up the many colours in Tulips & Roses, from the vibrant purple of phlox to the pinks of snapdragons and roses.

When we converted Tulips & Roses into an all-over pink version, the results were breathtakingly beautiful. Even though I say that about every monotone print we trial, this was the one that stole my heart. It found its way into my kitchen, where it replaced a set of curtains that had remained unchanged for the previous 15 years. The pink is feminine without being cloying and is the foundation of a charming and elegant room. I trimmed the inside length of each curtain with a handmade cotton fringe that mirrors the colours in the fabric exactly.

I have always loved the idea of lining curtains with a contrasting print. In my kitchen I used the Metro design, which has simple drawn lines interspersed with tiny floral motifs. Quiet and gentle, it is well suited to a secondary fabric role. It has also been used to cover the window seat cushion, and although it has been printed on a lighter base cloth of white linen, the two complement each other beautifully.

When we invented Constance, it required 12 separate screens to be made, but we considered it well worth the expense. Heavenly full-blown roses make up posies with a variety of other flowers in a palette of dark greens, faint pinks, deep maroons, yellows and purples. It represented something of a departure from our usual style, but there is a refined elegance in her cornucopia of exuberant colours.

PAGES 122–123 Our Toile de Poulet wallpaper in berry red makes for a particularly cozy and charming bedroom at the Priory in Somerset. A selection of multi-coloured Staffordshire figures has found a home on a side table. The Toile de Poulet pattern continues onto the linen curtains, which are hung from a painted curtain pole with wooden tie-backs. The blue-grey paint on the woodwork takes the pink edge off the room, giving it a smart and solid appearance, while the window seat and shutters echo the background of the stone-coloured fabric.

PREVIOUS PAGES Another view of the Toile de Poulet bedroom. The bed hangings were made by Maria Checkley, expertly measured by Monique Tacon and patiently hung by Jack Taylor. A matching eiderdown completes the Toile de Poulet experience, with plain white bedding to relieve the eye.

OPPOSITE The diminutive windows in this bedroom at Brook Cottage called for a grand curtain treatment. These drapes, made from Constance in the raspberry colourway, were rescued from our shop in Cambridge when it closed many years ago, hence the excessive length. On the bench are a pair of cushions – one in matching Constance and the other in Belmont, a now-discontinued pattern that may well be revived one day.

The original inspiration for Constance was a small, raggedy piece of cloth found at a French brocante. Parts of the pattern were so faded as to make them invisible. We handed over the fragment to the art department of our printers in the Lake District to fill in the empty spaces and make a full pattern repeat. It took days and days to perfect the colours, which are just the right side of faded, just the right side of bright. It was an exhausting and time-consuming process, leading to self-doubt and fear of settling on the wrong shades just to keep the peace. In the end, it is always worth the effort to get things just right. What I love about Constance is its femininity and its dreamlike quality, which works equally well in a living room or in a bedroom, in the city or in the country.

A fabric named Bees – featuring posies of roses adorned with garlands – was our first print and its faded green and coral-pink blooms are ideally suited to bedroom curtains. The gently faded and worn print gives the impression that the fabric has been inherited from a distant relative and carefully preserved over the years.

OPPOSITE AND ABOVE India Rose, based on an 18th-century oriental design, works just as well in a contemporary New York loft as in a Georgian priory.

OVERLEAF The small windows in my kitchen are framed beautifully by curtains made from Tulips & Roses and a window seat cushion in Metro, both in pink. Bounty from the garden is displayed in a French enamel coffee pot.

OPPOSITE Generously full-length curtains printed with the Elgin motif on natural
linen combine elegance with warmth. This close-up from a marathon four-day
photoshoot reveals the lovely texture and shaded printing in the pattern.
ABOVE A curtain made from our beautiful Alderney floral fabric printed in
soft pink and lined with striped pink Metro, both printed on a linen base cloth.

ABOVE LEFT For many years we have been working on a pink version of our bestselling blue fabric Mary, and at last we have achieved the desired result, as seen on this curtain. The foliage is the palest sage green while the roses are a strong yet gentle pink. RIGHT The Julia design features delicate medallions of floral posies in vertical rows. OPPOSITE Constance in her original multi-coloured incarnation makes a perfect country-house fabric.

On the Table

Tables play a large part in my life as a stylist, designer and homemaker. Some of my tables at home are too beautiful to cover with a cloth, while others will never be seen undressed. The joy of a tablecloth is that it can totally transform a room, bringing new colours, a new mood and a whole range of different decorative objects to show off.

A table positioned behind a sofa is an excellent surface on which to place a pair of lamps and to exhibit books, framed photographs, flowers and, in my case, an extensive collection of Staffordshire figures.

The beauty of being able to cover a table with a cloth is that it matters not what lurks beneath, it can be as simple as a piece of wood sitting on a pair of trestles.

A round table is a luxurious excuse to custom make an interlined covering that reaches the floor. Whether tucked into a corner of a room or placed centrally in an entrance hall, here is a marvellous pretext to present a welcoming display. Large pots and vases of seasonal flowers or, when there are no flowers, beautiful twigs entwined with twinkling lights, will help you establish a convivial and festive scene whatever the season.

Our linen tablecloths and napkins are always washed and tumbled before sale to give them a pre-loved, crumpled appearance, which I always find much more homely than a starched linen tablecloth.

LEFT Pink Tulips & Roses fabric on a round table with a black and white vintage tole lamp, a black tin box and matching candles. OPPOSITE Curtains in Meggernie and a raspberry Hatley cushion flanked by two cushions in pink Tulips & Roses and pink India Rose, which match the lampshades behind them.

OVERLEAF A cottage breakfast scene with Meggernie curtains in the background and a Tulips and Roses tablecloth made from washed and tumbled linen. Flowers from the garden are displayed in an old galvanized bucket.

A Life Outdoors

INSPIRING SCHEMES FOR INVITING OUTDOOR SPACES

Flowers and foliage, inside and out, are essential ingredients for appealing rooms and gardens. I have discovered that a simple colour palette in the garden calms the visual outlook and creates an undemanding landscape of great beauty.

The moment when cow parsley, also known as Queen Anne's lace, springs to life in the hedgerows is a joyful event. Its gigantic sprigs of charming blooms are swiftly brought inside and placed in vases in every room of the house. I then turn to delicate *Ammi majus*, which I sow twice a year to ensure a succession of blooms all summer long.

Bringing fabrics outdoors is a wonderful way to extend your interior decoration into the garden. It is as well to plan your planting so that it co-ordinates with your chosen palette, but white flowers and green or silver leaves are especially versatile. They look lovely when paired with fabrics in charcoal tones and can also brave yellows, pinks and lilacs.

Charcoal Stripes

Many of our fabrics look perfectly at home in the great outdoors. For an entirely new twist, we recently experimented with a bold charcoal stripe printed onto a white linen ground. Although this pattern is a definite departure from our usual faded florals and gentle stripes, it has made a strikingly beautiful cloth for this long outdoor table. The colours work well with the green and white of a summer garden, especially this one, in which the dark courtyard pool reflects the charcoal of the fabric. Black pots of beautiful silvery-grey lavender, waiting to be planted, provide more greyscale accents. Next year these lavender plants will have white flowers – further accentuating the simple colour scheme.

As a stylist, I am always thinking about what the camera will see – whether the colours and shapes will jar or enhance one another. I find that sticking to a cohesive palette, sometimes even down to the food, makes it much easier to create a dramatic and striking setting. In this garden, the white flowers and green foliage make a great impact with the charcoal and white stripes. On the table, the green grapes and gigantic white bowls of bright green lettuce are as decorative as any flower. In the winter months, fresh herbs in pots – especially silvery sage, thyme and rosemary – are more readily available than flowers and look lovely inside and out.

PREVIOUS PAGE A view of the garden at Brook Cottage and its much-loved outdoor pavilion under a blue sky.

THIS PAGE AND OPPOSITE This generously gathered tablecloth in our graphic Three-Inch Stripe has been made to fit the garden table exactly. The simple chairs have been dressed in matching covers. The greenery in the garden and the vibrant salad leaves enhance the charcoal tones.

OVERLEAF Just four colours make up this striking image photographed in the courtyard of a magnificent Georgian house in the English countryside. The charcoal-striped linen was chosen to enhance the beautiful black-lined plunge pool, the canopy supports and the black garden bench. The colour palette of the planting consists of entirely white, silver and green.

Blues and Lilacs

All of our various blue colourways have a serene, timeless feel. Each one is a gentle friend that demands little attention, but brings a comforting and demure ambience to an outdoor setting.

Living in the UK, my instincts tend to lead me to pink-toned fabrics, which are forgiving under grey skies. However, blue fabrics can also look very lovely, even when there is no blue sky for them to reflect. The sparsely spaced roses of blue Hatley on a crisp white ground are heart-stoppingly beautiful when used to cover a lunchtime table.

My first book, *Vintage Chic*, featured a photograph of a simple tent made from printed cotton canvas, which was held up by a washing line in the dappled shade of two trees beside a babbling brook. The enduring appeal of this photograph, first published nearly 20 years ago, proves that lovely design will endure beyond what is fashionable and transient. The blues, with their affinity for water, slip gently into lilac, and the greenery of an English summer garden becomes the fortification and consort of this much-neglected shade.

RIGHT In the garden at Brook Cottage, *Ammi majus* is grown in abundance. Planning the cutting garden in the winter months ensures a constant supply of flowers and foliage throughout the year. OPPOSITE This is image from my first book *Vintage Chic*, which came out in 2003. A piece of canvas, printed with our Hatley design in blue, was thrown over a washing line and weighted with stones to make a charming tent.

OVERLEAF The Brook Cottage garden has many seating areas to take full advantage of the sun as it moves throughout the day. This table is set for a light luncheon by the pool with a tablecloth in blue Hatley. A vintage basket is filled with garden flowers and the ferns that grow wild on the country lanes.

By this English swimming pool, lunch is laid out on a blue Hatley linen tablecloth, bringing to mind Mediterranean holidays, good food and blue skies. Perhaps this is why the colour blue is perceived as a happy colour: serene and fresh, for many of us it is a reminder of warm weather and happy times by the sea. Perfectly suited to a summer lunch, blue Hatley is summer personified.

With their tendency to crumple and their magical ability to make one feel cool in the heat and warm in the cold, our linen fabrics are ideally suited to outdoor spaces and will help you create a relaxed, summery ambience. The fabric will soften over time and become more beautiful with each wash, especially when left to air dry.

THIS PAGE AND OPPOSITE The old galvanized garden table is dressed for tea with a lilac Hatley linen tablecloth. I do love a lilac and green theme. Hostas are fleeting and unpredictable, but at the moment of photography we were blessed with their flowers in full bloom. Lavender and sweet peas decorate the table, along with a selection of pink lustreware cups and saucers.

Most of the colours in our fabric and wallpaper collections have been inspired by hues found in nature, and our lilac colourway. is no exception. This glorious lilac tablecloth, in the Hatley design, was an absolute joy to style, with the perfectly timed hostas offering up their short-lived flowers just in time for our photography. Not to mention the divine sweet peas and lavender flowers with their delicate scent and colour – seen against the lush greenery growing on the walls of Brook Cottage, they demonstrate just how harmoniously lilac and green work together. An assortment of delicate mauve china from

my collection was brought out to complete the table decoration, demonstrating that the interior and exterior colour palettes can and should be regarded as one and the same.

Neither contemporary nor old fashioned, lilac is welcome in any situation and adds just enough colour to be enchanting, even in an urban environment, or with grey winter skies. It was once the grandest, rarest colour in the world, the preserve of royalty alone, so we are fortunate to have access to this wonderful shade today.

Rose Tinted

So thrilled are we British at the, mostly rare, sight of sunshine, it is our habit to decant the inside to the outside at the first hint of summer. Here in my pavilion, whatever the weather, we diligently become outdoor people, breakfasting, lunching and dining there throughout the season.

It is furnished with an Old Rocker swing seat from Brigette Buchanan's company, ODD Limited. I have endowed this with eiderdown seat covers and a multitude of Cabbages & Roses cushions. The prints vary, but they work well together because they share the same tone of pink. From the elegant Charlotte fabric on the table to ditzy Catherine Rose on the seat, to Podge on the cushions, this hotchpotch of designs lends an air of friendliness. Being exposed to the damp and rainy climate, alternating with strong sunshine, our furnishings in the pavilion do tend to fade, but this is all part of the Cabbages & Roses attitude of relaxed imperfection.

The range of our pink fabrics is varied – in my garden, the extravagantly drawn Charlotte in raspberry makes an appearance as tablecloths, on which the beauty of the print can be examined closely rather than seen from afar on a curtain. The generous bouquets of old-fashioned roses are finely drawn with a background of picotage dots shading the base cloth. Both the pink and raspberry colours are perfectly suited to the outside, where they complement the green of the countryside and the pink roses that can be seen flourishing in the distance. Here again, it is as well to have a planting plan that reflects the fabrics used inside and outside.

The rose version of Charlotte, photographed in the outside pavilion, also makes a lovely tablecloth; unassuming and gentle, it leaves plenty of scope to add decorative touches when setting the table. The pure white weave of the linen brings an atmosphere of old-fashioned respectability and demureness to the setting.

OPPOSITE The Old Rocker inside the pavilion is dressed with a multitude of cushions in pink Cabbages & Roses fabrics, including Podge and Catherine Rose. The seat is softened with washable quilts, also in the Catherine Rose design. ABOVE A duvet cover, made from Alderney in raspberry, airs on the wooden balustrade.

OVERLEAF LEFT A bench offers up an abundance of all-important candles, with Bees – our very first fabric design – in the background. RIGHT A table inside the pavilion is set for lunch with a pretty tablecloth in the Bees print.

PAGES 156–157 The pavilion is a much-used room where we enjoy most of our meals throughout the summer, whatever the weather.

THIS PAGE AND OPPOSITE The glorious pink Charlotte fabric covers the table inside the pavilion, where pink roses are used as table decoration all summer long.

OVERLEAF This table under the dappled shade of the willow tree provides another location for a tea party extravaganza. The table is covered in Charlotte in raspberry.

"Both the pink and raspberry colours are perfectly suited to the outside, where they complement the green of the countryside and the pink roses that can be seen flourishing in the distance."

OPPOSITE AND ABOVE Details from the tea party, with linen napkins and posies of flowers from the garden displayed on the Charlotte linen tablecloth. The antique knives and forks gleam in the dappled sunlight.

OVERLEAF This magical tent, which covered our courtyard for 10 years, was a perfect space for entertaining – and for showing off Cabbages & Roses' fabrics.

Lilac Pink

Jonquil *

Cuisse de
Nymphe Emue *

C&R

ck *

Lavender

Rose

Nicaragua

Tyrian

CABBAGES & ROSES

Fabric Ranges

FLORALS, DOTS, STRIPES AND WALLPAPERS

All of Cabbages & Roses' fabrics and wallpapers have been invented, re-invented, re-coloured and re-scaled over the past 20 years. New colours have been added here and there, allowing us to keep up with the times.

The collection, pictured on the following pages, has grown organically to meet the needs of our customers. Now that we have, at last, found our feet, I expect we shall be working for the next 20 years on different fabrics to fill another book, and to furnish and embellish our homes.

Who knows where we will be in 2042, but let us hope that we will have surmounted the enormous problems we are facing today, and that we will have learned to tread gently on the earth by choosing, manufacturing and buying sustainably and beautifully.

FLORALS AND DOTS

ALDERNEY
NATURAL

Blossom

Charcoal

French Blue

Grey

Pink

Raspberry

Teal

ALDERNEY

Blue

Charcoal

Dove

Pink

Raspberry

BEES

Multi

CATHERINE ROSE

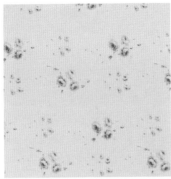 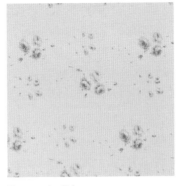 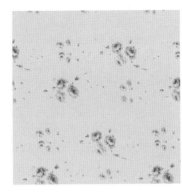

Blue

French Blue

Pink

CHARLOTTE

Blue

Charcoal

Dove

French Blue

Lilac

Pink

Rose

CONSTANCE NATURAL

Charcoal

French Blue

Multi

CONSTANCE NATURAL

Continued

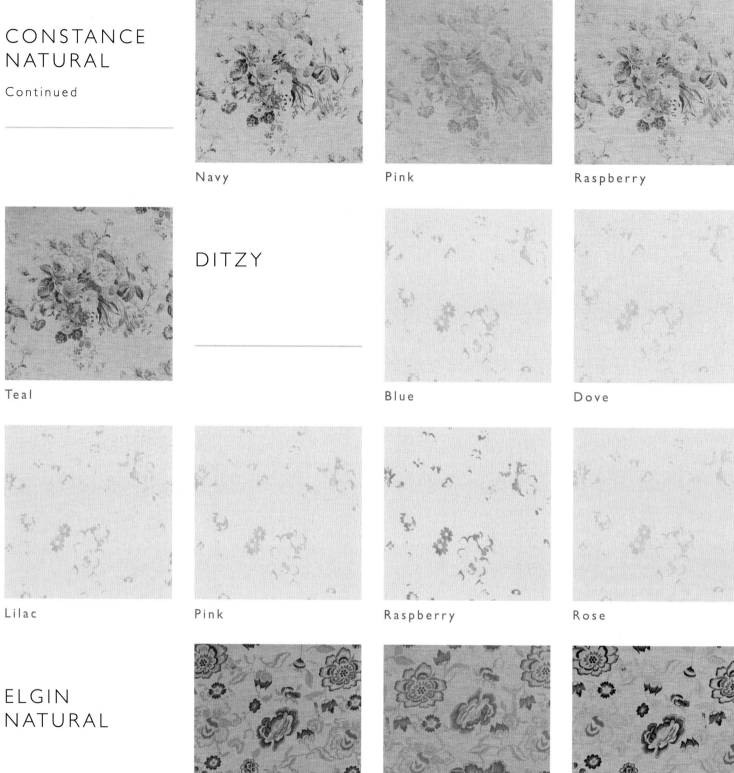

Navy

Pink

Raspberry

Teal

DITZY

Blue

Dove

Lilac

Pink

Raspberry

Rose

ELGIN NATURAL

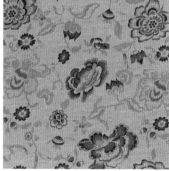

Charcoal

French Blue

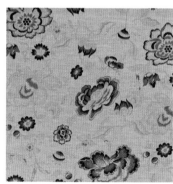

Navy

ELGIN NATURAL

Continued

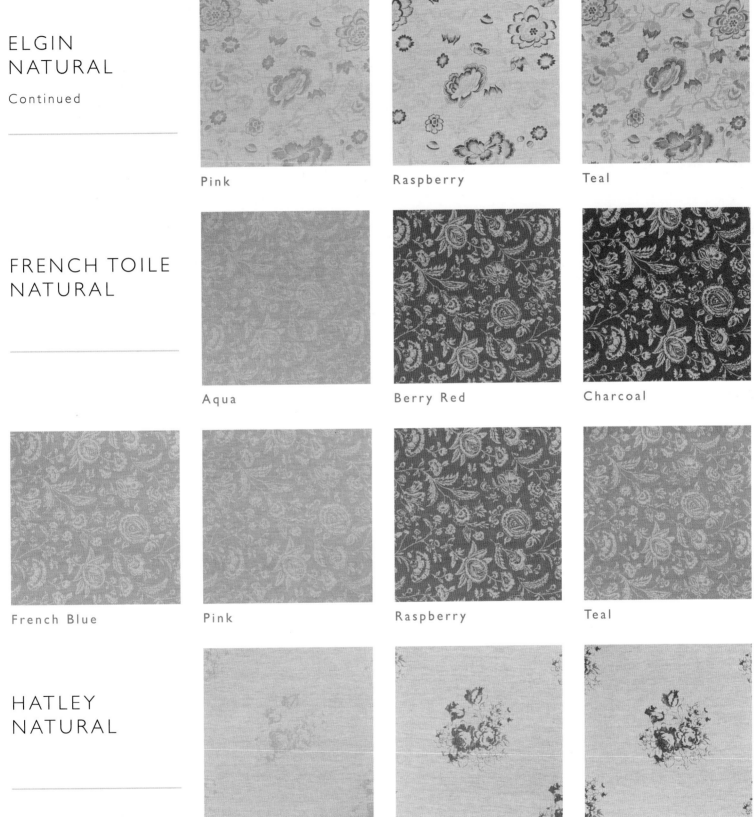

Pink

Raspberry

Teal

FRENCH TOILE NATURAL

Aqua

Berry Red

Charcoal

French Blue

Pink

Raspberry

Teal

HATLEY NATURAL

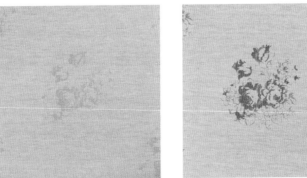

Aqua

Berry Red

Charcoal

HATLEY
NATURAL

Continued

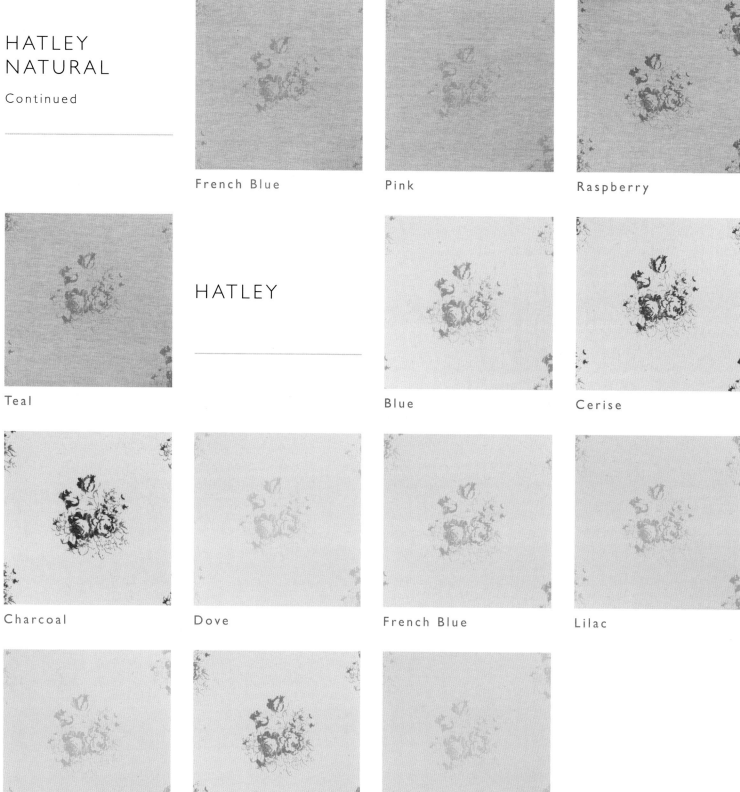

French Blue

Pink

Raspberry

Teal

HATLEY

Blue

Cerise

Charcoal

Dove

French Blue

Lilac

Pink

Raspberry

Rose

INDIA ROSE NATURAL

Charcoal

French Blue

Multi

Navy

Pink

Teal

JULIA

Blue

Charcoal

Dove

French Blue

Lilac

Pink

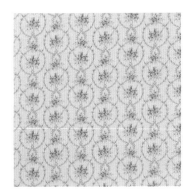
Raspberry

MARY NATURAL

Floral Multi

French Blue

Pink

MEGGERNIE NATURAL

  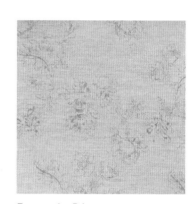

Berry Red

Charcoal

French Blue

Pink

Raspberry

Teal

MEGGERNIE

  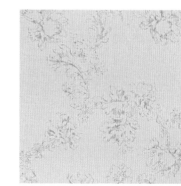

Blue

Charcoal

Dove

MEGGERNIE

Continued

Lilac

Pink

Raspberry

METRO NATURAL

Aqua

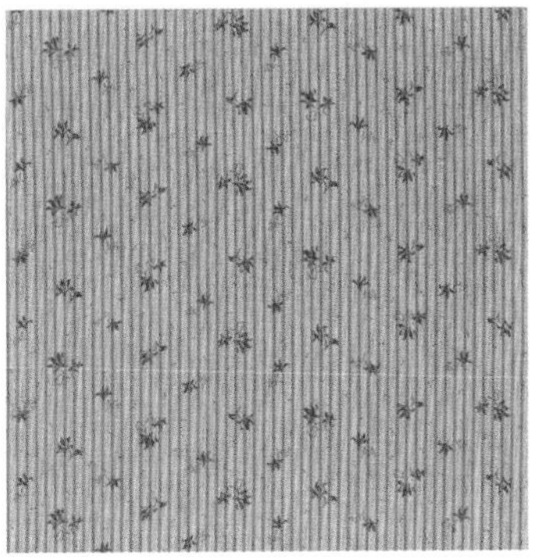

Berry Red

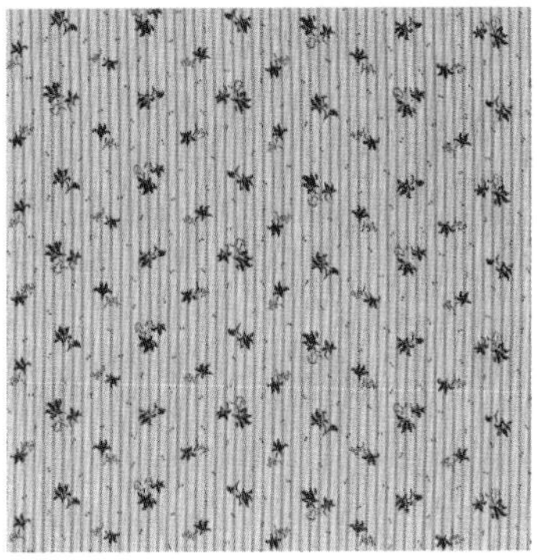

Charcoal

French Blue

Pink

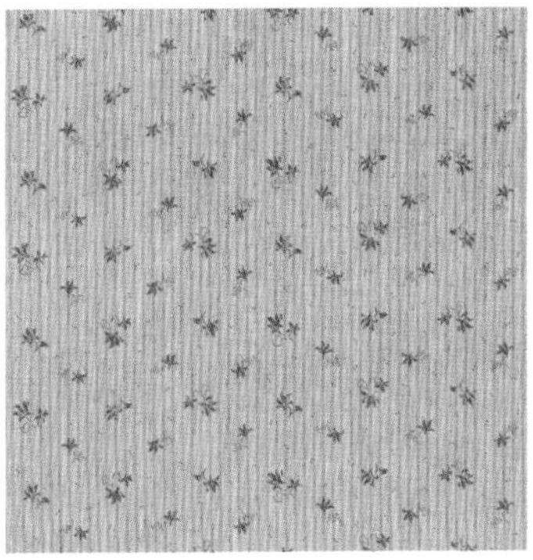

Raspberry

Teal

METRO

Blue

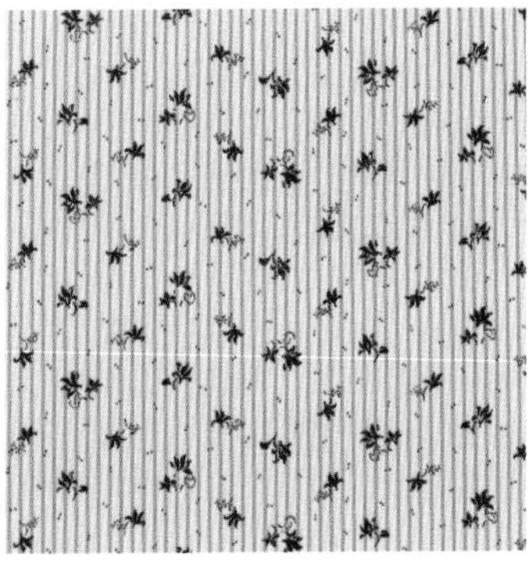

Charcoal

Dove

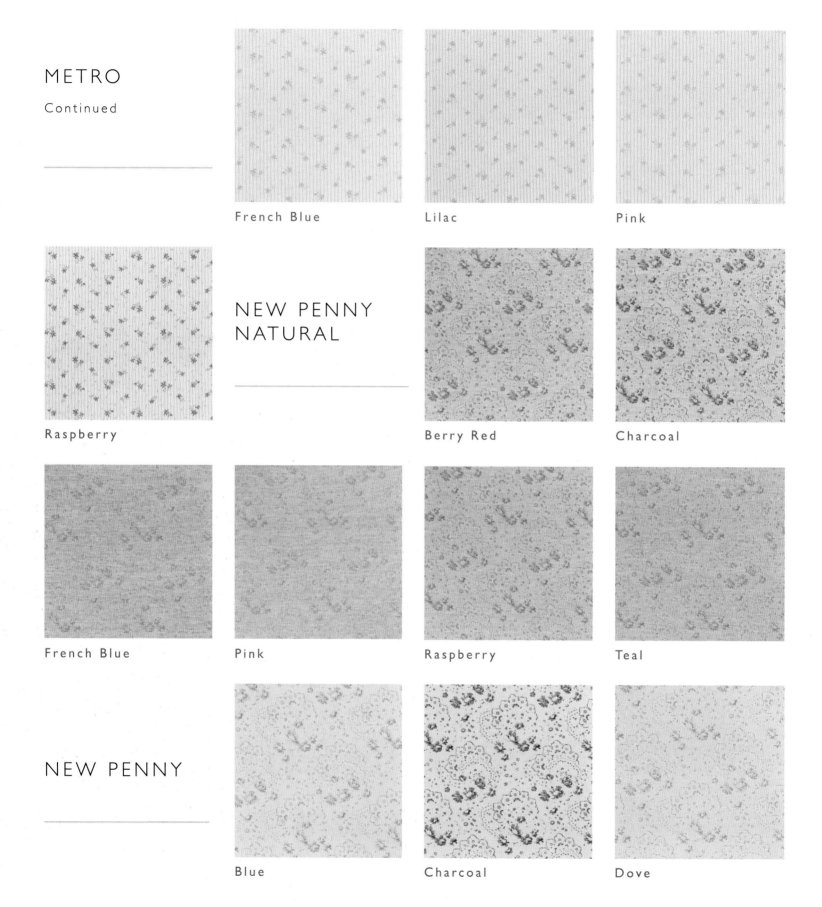

METRO

Continued

French Blue

Lilac

Pink

Raspberry

NEW PENNY
NATURAL

Berry Red

Charcoal

French Blue

Pink

Raspberry

Teal

NEW PENNY

Blue

Charcoal

Dove

NEW PENNY

Continued

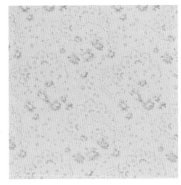 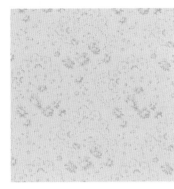 

French Blue — Lilac — Pink

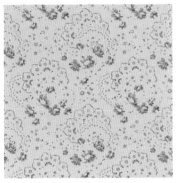 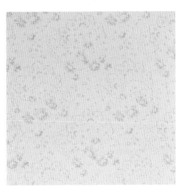

Raspberry — Rose

PARIS ROSE NATURAL

Berry Red — Charcoal — French Blue

Pink — Raspberry — Teal

PODGE

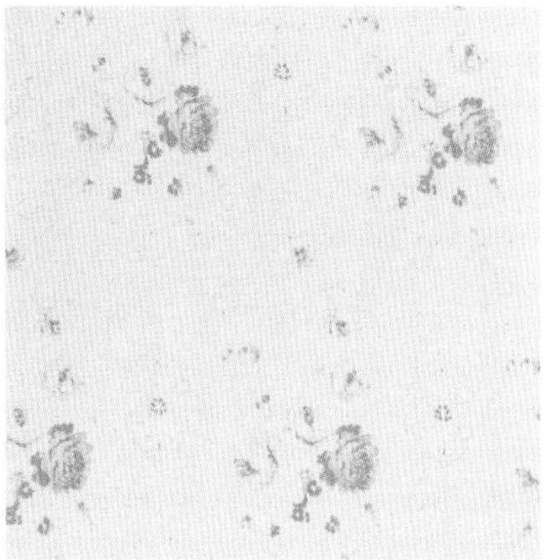

Blue

Dove

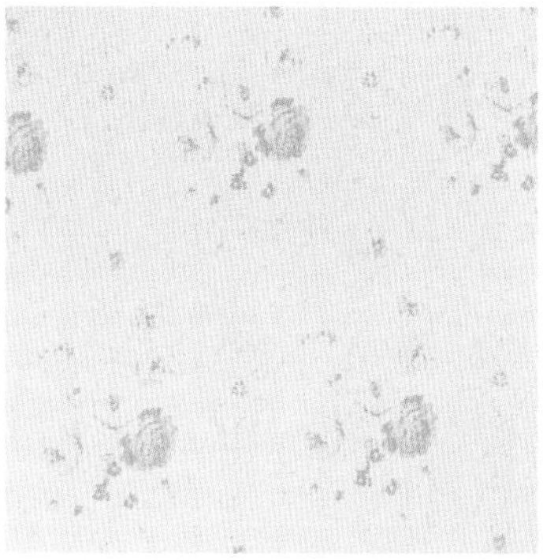

Lilac

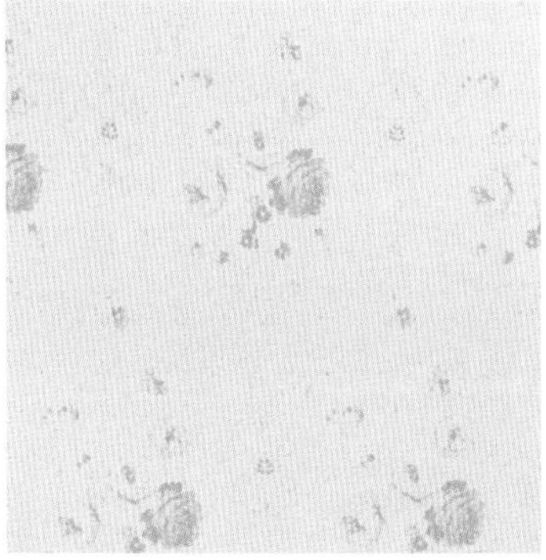

Pink

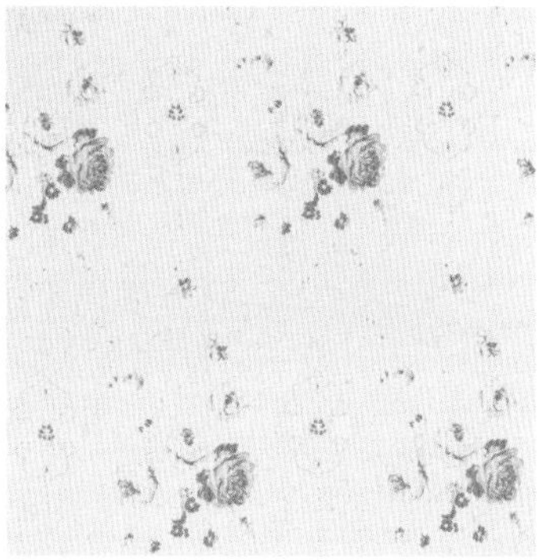

Raspberry

PROVENCE
TOILE
NATURAL

Aqua

Berry Red

Charcoal

French Blue

Pink

Raspberry

Teal

ROSIE

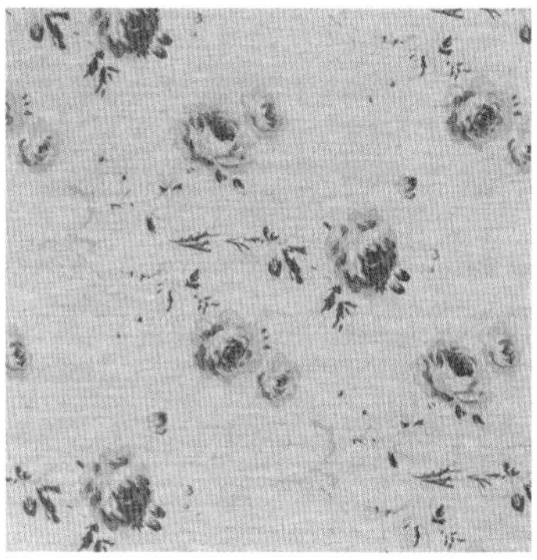

Raspberry

SCOOPY
NATURAL

Aqua

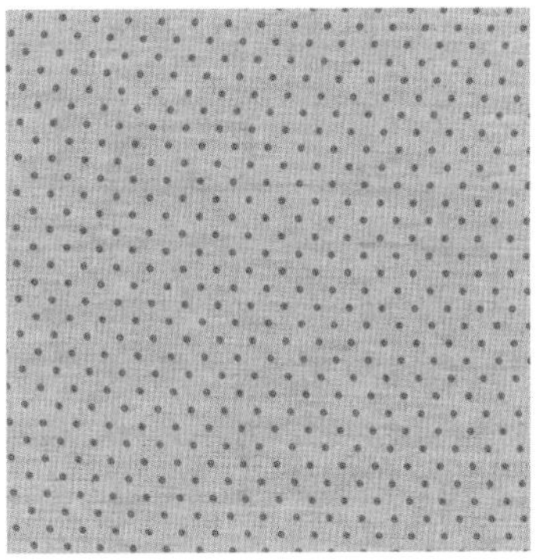

Berry Red

Charcoal

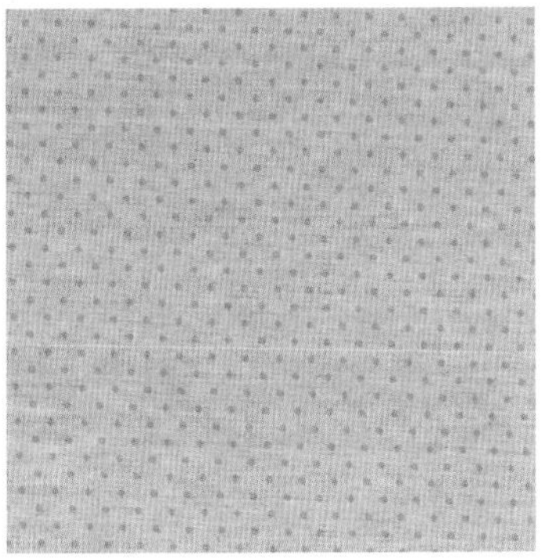

French Blue

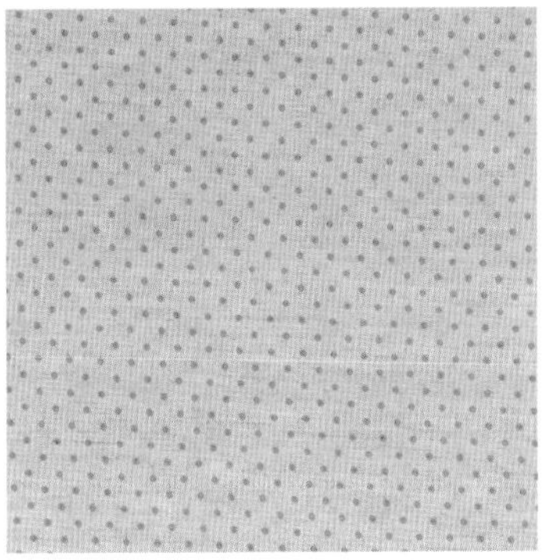

Pink

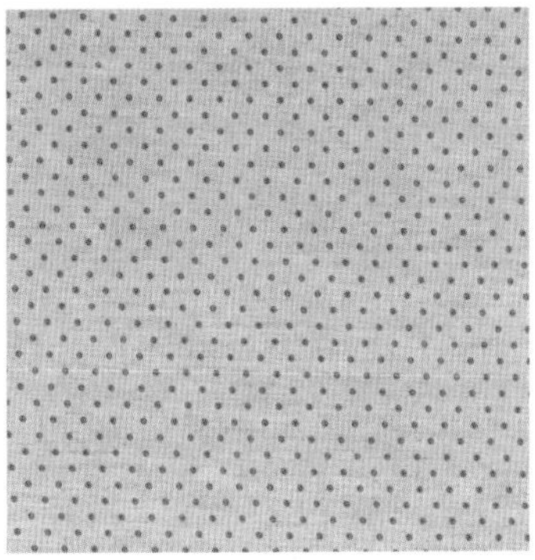

Raspberry

Teal

TOILE DE
POULET
NATURAL

Berry Red

Charcoal

French Blue

Pink

Raspberry

Teal

TULIPS
AND ROSES
NATURAL

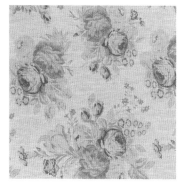

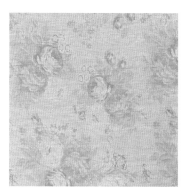

Charcoal

Multi

Pink

STRIPES

JOLLY STRIPE
NATURAL

Aqua

Berry Red

Charcoal

French Blue

Navy

Pink

Raspberry

JOLLY STRIPE NATURAL

Continued

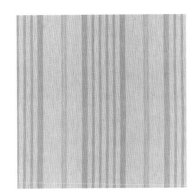

Teal

THREE INCH STRIPE

Blue

Charcoal

Dove

French Blue

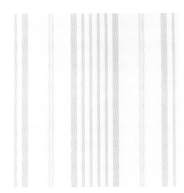

Lilac

Pink

Raspberry

Rose

THREE INCH STRIPE NATURAL

Aqua

Berry Red

Charcoal

French Blue

Navy

Pink

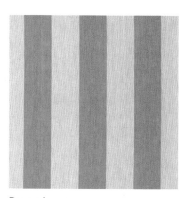

Raspberry

Teal

THRE INCH STRIPE

Blue

Charcoal

Dove

French Blue

Lilac

Pink

THREE INCH STRIPE

Continued

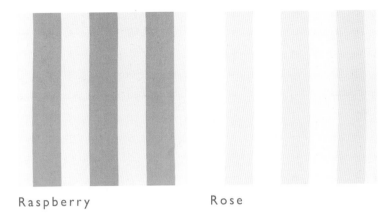

Raspberry   Rose

WALLPAPERS

ALDERNEY
WALLPAPER

Raspberry

CATHERINE
ROSE
WALLPAPER

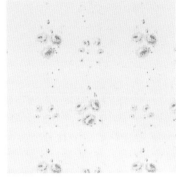

Blue

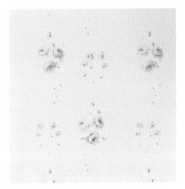

Pink

HATLEY
WALLPAPER

Pink

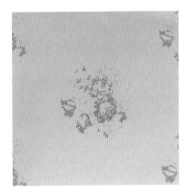

Dove

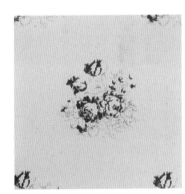

Black

PARIS ROSE
WALLPAPER

French Blue

USEFUL INSTAGRAM ACCOUNTS

FABRICS & WALLPAPERS

Cabbages & Roses @cabbages_and_roses

PAINTS

Bauwerk Colour
@bauwerkcolour

Edward Bulmer Natural Paint
@edwardbulmerpaints

Farrow & Ball
@farrowandball

Little Greene
@littlegreenepaintco

Paint & Paper Library
@paintandpaperlibrary

VINTAGE

C'est Tout Interiors
@cesttoutinteriors

Chalk & Paisley
@chalkandpaisley

Lacquer Chest
@lacquerchest

Little Wren Vintage
@littlewrenvintage

Natalia Violet Antiques
@nataliavioletantiques

Stenvall Interiors
@stenvall_interiors

The Country Brocante
@thecountrybrocante

INTERIORS

Berdoulat
@berdoulat_interior_design

Emma Burns
@violetburns

Jack Property Maintenance
@jackpropmain

Liz Morris Decorative Interiors
@lizmorrisdecorativeinteriors

Pale & Interesting
@paleandinterestingstore

Sugar & Spice
@sugarandspicefurnishings

GARDENS & FLOWERS

A Bunch of Wild
@abunchofwild

Black Shed Flower Farm
@blackshedflowers

David Austin Roses
@david_austin_roses

Farmer Gracy
@farmergracy

Honeysuckle & Hilda
@honeysuckle_and_hilda

Kitten Grayson Flowers
@kittengraysonflowers

Petersham Nurseries
@petershamnurseries

Psalter Farm Flowers
@psalterfarmflowers

The Land Gardeners
@thelandgardeners

Wild Willow Flowers
@wildwillowflowers

Willow Crossley
@willowcrossleycreates

FURNITURE & ACCESSORIES

Byron & Byron
@byronandbyron

Farm Soap Co
@farmsoapco

ODD Limited
@odd_limited

Pinch
@pinch_london

Transpontine Books
@transpontinebooks

CERAMICS

Georgia Loizou Ceramics
@georgialoizouceramics

Joseph Dupré
@josephduprestudios

Pollyanna Johnson Ceramics
@pollyannajohnsonceramics

Polly Fern
@pollyfern

MAGAZINES

Country Living
@countrylivinguk

Gardens Illustrated
@gardens_illustrated

Homes & Gardens
@homesandgardens

House & Garden
@houseandgardenuk

The World of Interiors
@theworldofinteriors

INSPIRATIONAL ACCOUNTS

Alexandra Tolstoy
@alexandratolstoy

Arthur Parkinson
@arthurparkinson_

Belle Daughtry
@just_belle

Bible of British Taste
@bibleofbritishtaste

Hill House Vintage
@hillhousevintage

Inigo
@inigo.house

Violet Dent
@violet_dent

PHOTOGRAPHERS

Cover James Scott-Long
2-4 James Scott-Long
5 Annabelle Daughtry
6 Lucinda Symons
8-9 Edina van der Wyck
10-11 Belle Daughtry
12 top Lucinda Symons
12 bottom Annabelle Daughtry
13-14 Andrew Beasley
15-19 Belle Daughtry
20 James Scott-Long
22-23 Belle Daughtry
25 Courtesy of Ashley Wilde
26 Simon Brown
27 Lucinda Symons
28-29 Belle Daughtry
30 Antony Crolla
31 Andrew Beasley
32-34 Belle Daughtry

35 left Simon Brown
35 right Belle Daughtry
36-38 James Scott-Long
39 Edina van der Wyck
40 left James Scott-Long
40 right Lucinda Symons
41-43 James Scott-Long
45 Belle Daughtry
46 left Andrew Beasley
46 right
47-51 James Scott-Long
53 left James Scott-Long
53 right Belle Daughtry
54-55 Andrew Beasley
56 left James Scott-Long
56 right Lucinda Symons
57 Belle Daughtry
58-61 Andrew Beasley
62 James Scott-Long

64-65 Belle Daughtry
66-68 James Scott-Long
69 left Antony Crolla
69 right James Scott-Long
70-71 Simon Brown
72 James Scott-Long
73 Andrew Beasley
74 Simon Brown
75-88 James Scott-Long
89 Antony Crolla
90-91 Andrew Beasley
91 right Belle Daughtry
92-93 James Scott-Long
94-95 Andrew Beasley
96-99 Belle Daughtry
100 James Scott-Long
101-105 Belle Daughtry
106-107 Lucinda Symons
108-111 Belle Daughtry

112-113 Andrew Beasley
114 Antony Crolla
115-121 James Scott-Long
122-125 Belle Daughtry
127 Andrew Beasley
128 James Scott-Long
129 Edina van der Wyck
130-131 Belle Daughtry
132-139 James Scott-Long
140-146 Belle Daughtry
147 Edina van der Wyck
148-163 Belle Daughtry
164-165 Edina van der Wyck
166 Belle Daughtry
183 bottom Andrew Beasley
184 Belle Daughtry
186
187-191 James Scott-Long

INDEX

ACKNOWLEDGMENTS

There are many that I owe a huge debt of gratitude to who, for more than two decades, have supported and stood by Cabbages & Roses (and me). Our Cabbage Roses, in various roles at various times, have come and gone, and so have numerous photographers, designers, sewers, advisors and friends who have contributed to this book, which in reality has taken 22 years to make. So, in no particular order, but with such thanks to all…

My husband Mark Strutt for putting up with long absences over the years. My friend and inspiration Brigette Buchanan, who came on the first journey with me, and her daughter Violet Dent, both of whom continue to steadfastly champion and contribute to Cabbages & Roses. All the photographers whose photographs were chosen from so many that made this book: James Scott-Long, Belle Daughtry, Simon Brown, Edina van der Wyck and Andrew Beasley. Belle has also worked in numerous roles within the company during her young life. The current Cabbage Roses, particularly Monique Tacon, a mother to us all.

To all the printers of fabric and wallpapers, but particularly Howard Voyce (aka Podge), who is always so generous with his knowledge about all things print. Louise Hatley, our first teacher and collaborator.

To Simon Nagy and his team for their endless patience. To Maria Checkley of Sugar & Spice, who magically produced complicated and beautiful furnishings at the drop of a hat, and to Jack Taylor and his expertise in fixing said furnishings. Thank you to Simon Lewis, who has wallpapered endless walls at the drop of a hat for Cabbages & Roses Thank you to Tiffany Dunlop for her lovely drawings, which grace this page of the book. To Maria Gibbs for keeping our beautiful shop running smoothly. Thank you to Cindy Richards who commissioned our first book and this, probably our last, and to Sally Powell and Sophie Devlin for their expertise in book design and editing. An enormous thank you to Rian Davies, who was so patient and so brilliant in designing the book, and who put up with our filing system of photographs without a word of complaint. To all our customers who have supported us for 22 turbulent years.

But most of all to my daughter and her husband, Kate and Christopher Howells, whose patience, generosity and sheer brilliance in keeping the company thriving are genuinely astounding – for that I thank you.

Christina Strutt